C000186448

ONE EGG
OR TWO

ONE EGG OR TWO

20 Years an Army Chef

Paul Rowcliffe

One Egg or Two was originally published in 1995
by Lindsay Ross Publishing

This edition first published in the
United Kingdom in 2020 by Cavalcade Books

www.cavalcadebooks.com

© Paul Rowcliffe 1995, 2020

The moral right of the author has been asserted.
All rights reserved.

No part of this publication may be reproduced, stored in a
retrieval system or transmitted, in any form or by any means,
without the prior permission in writing of the publisher, nor
be otherwise circulated in any form of binding or cover other
than that in which it is published and without a similar
condition including this condition being imposed on the
subsequent purchaser.

ISBN 978-1-8381490-1-7

Cover design by Martin Bushell

To my daughter, Lisa

CONTENTS

CHAPTER 1

The cold windy platform of Exeter St. David's Station seemed the loneliest place on earth to the person about to board the train, even though he had all the family around him, preparing themselves for a tearful send off. For no reason other than the fact that he felt it was the right thing to do, he was about to embark on a career which was to span twenty years, and bring so many pleasant and unpleasant times that he would one day be able to sit his grandchildren on his knee and fascinate them for hours. For a 15-year-old that was a fair way off; still, it doesn't hurt to dream.

The train pulled into the platform and the three-hour journey to Aldershot was about to begin. I bade farewell to the family knowing that for the next six weeks I was on my own. What if I can't take it? Can I look after myself? These and many other questions were whizzing through my head as the guard blew his whistle and the 08.10 started to pull slowly out of the station.

I was alone for the first time ever except for my fellow travellers, who all looked as though they had been making the journey for years, and considering that this was the Penzance to London train they probably had. That was except the one leaning against the window of the compartment who looked as though he was as confused as I was. I asked where he was heading, which, now that I look back, was very forward of me. The reply was coincidental to say the least; 'Aldershot' he said with a somewhat troubled look! 'To join up?' I asked. The reply was a positive one. 'Army Catering Corps,' he said. 'Ha!' I said, 'me too.'

After the initial introduction and several minutes of trivial chatter, I realised that perhaps making new friends was not going to be as much of a problem as I had first imagined. Tony was as worried as I was about the life that we had chosen to embark upon, but the old saying of 'a trouble shared' was somewhat relevant in this case.

The train pulled in and out of several stations and I kept getting glimpses of the small suitcase that housed all my belongings and which always sent my mind flowing back to the family I had left on the station. Father had prepared me for the worst with the stories of his National Service back in 1952. If it was going to be like he said, then this was to be no picnic.

Tales of kit inspections were paramount in my mind. What were tankers? Would I know the R.S.M.

at first sight as had been suggested or is he like God and invisible? Could any human being be as bad as the stories I had heard?

I had lessons on all sorts of subjects in order to prepare me for 'A Man's Life' in the Army, like the badges of rank, how to determine whether to salute or not (I mean I would look rather silly saluting a Corporal), how to 'bull' up my boots. Oh! how I wished I had taken it in more; I know I should have listened, but I knew better. But I thought it must have changed since Father's time, surely.

I was about to be brought home to reality – the train was pulling into Aldershot Station after a quick change at Woking. This was it, the start of what was to become six weeks' torture.

As we disembarked from the carriage, there was a group of around twenty long-haired youths gathering just outside the main door of the platform. As I handed my ticket to the uniformed collector and was shunted through the door, I took a couple of minutes to gather my thoughts and then realised the group, getting larger by the minute, was the one I had to join. I handed in my paperwork and we were shunted on to the back of a draughty four-ton truck that had obviously seen better days, as had the Palace Cinema that we were passing en route to our new home, St. Omer Barracks.

The whole complex was dominated by a tall office building, which was to send shivers up the back of many a brave man as he journeyed back to

Aldershot to extend his training and experience. This great landmark was to become known as 'The Tower Block', and I can tell you that the sight of this twelve-floored monster has been known to reduce the strongest man to a quivering wreck, though this was unknown to us 'sproggs' who were newly arrived at camp. But it was apparent that there was to be no lounging around; from the minute we drove through the camp gates it started. 'Line up there, move over here,' – it did not stop.

First introduction to our intake staff proved to be a real eye opener. The Sergeant who seemed to be at least eight-foot tall, and who pledged to be taking over from our mums, just did not have the same manner as we had been used to from dear old Mum and Dad. Still, we, in our trusting way, let him take us under his wing and before very long into our training had adorned him with the nickname of Daddy Plevin.

He really did have our welfare at heart because he did not want us to have the problem of washing long hair, so he showed us into a lovely looking shop with a big chair in the middle of the floor, and the sound of the shears buzzing with excitement at the thought of another forty-five civvies about to be transformed into the first stage of the typical squaddie.

First into the chair was a very brave young man – at this stage names do not really matter, but he asked for a No. 3, which, to the uninitiated, is a crew cut and, as we were all in the same boat, like a flock of sheep the majority including myself followed suit. This cut down the length of time for the ones still waiting. This I thought was slightly unfair tactics because it not only threw you in at the deep end but also gave you time to think about the mistakes you might well have made, but it was too late for me. Anyway, I was in to stay, even if it killed me, which at the moment looked highly probable. I just could not go home and get told by anyone who felt the urge that I couldn't take the pressure.

So here I was a three-hour train journey from the ones that I loved with the hair on my head already reduced from its former glory to a harsh spiky stubble, but it was a free haircut and I was by no means alone; the other 44 'nigs' (new intake) as we had been labelled so affectionately were all in the same boat.

After very little time we were being shaped and honed to fit the roles that all of us had chosen to fill. Instead of our casual saunter from the camp gates to the reception area, as was the case when we arrived, we were now more of a very untidy group moving under a Junior Non-Commissioned Officer. He was becoming more stressed by the minute and it showed by the volume of his vocal cords being raised to equal that of the fog horn on the Titanic, but he was having as much effect on us as the

Titanic did against the iceberg that was to ruin her maiden voyage. Still, at least the NCO had six weeks to keep us afloat.

The rooms that we were ushered into had a homely feel to them and were divided into two halves, each half housing four soldiers. I remembered one of the tips given to me by my father, and chose the bed furthest from the door, but the Corporal in charge of the room had his own ideas and I was immediately rehoused into the next bed. Oh Well! never mind, I did not really want the bed near the window anyway.

That evening we were entertained by various persons, each having his own area of responsibility and doing his utmost to ensure that we knew exactly what was about to become of the group now known as 'C Company'.

The alarm call in the shape of a large man in a strange-looking, green camouflaged suit wielding a pick axe shaft came bursting through the door at 05.30 and let out various obscenities to raise us from the semi-comfortable slumber that had not set in until around 3 a.m., so all was not roses when we eventually queued for our first taste of the typical Army breakfast. As we reached the chef who was serving the fried eggs, I am sure I was not the only one who wondered how many hours previous to this he, and the other members of his squad, had got up to lay on the large spread that lay before us.

We seemed to be the centre of attraction as the

initiated had been there some months already and their comments, obviously meant to frighten us out of our skins, were having the desired effect.

The lad in front of me nearly lost the use of his right hand as a half-pint ladle came slamming down on the container to his front with the bellow of the Shift Sergeant informing him that one rasher of bacon would probably be all he could eat – though the words used were a little more straightforward than that! But my friend agreed that he was not that hungry anyway.

This was definitely not the kind of breakfast that I was used to, and that included the company. Although we had all been introduced to each other and had chatted and discussed the lifestyle that lay before us, that was the only thing that any of us had in common.

The thirty minutes to wolf down a full English breakfast seemed to us slightly uncivilised. Whatever happened to the hour or so browsing through the newspaper? Even if the periodical had had just the page three photograph it would have seemed slightly pointless as there was no time to look at it.

We were herded like sheep outside the dining room and marched directly to the store that was to issue us with our first items of kit. We were just another group of no-hopers, or so it seemed by the reception that was to greet us from behind the four-foot-high wooden counter that had obviously seen more kit issues than breakfasts served in the whole of the complex. The somewhat ageing gentlemen who served us, if that's the right expression (and forgive me for being a little under-excited), had been issuing kit to the uninitiated since Monty was issued with his two cap badges.

The queue in front of me got shorter and my comrades-in-arms came out of the double doors barely able to balance with the huge pile of olive green (drab) clothing which, if you wanted to buy it, would probably be best found in the market by searching out the stall with the fewest customers. A large beige suitcase finished the issue, which only helped to fire up the discussion outside as to why the case had not been issued first so that we could put the kit in as it was issued; but then we were in the Army and they have their funny ways, as any ex-squaddie who reads this record will remember.

After being once again trooped back to the rooms that had now become home, we put all our newly issued garb into the lockers that were provided, but not as the black and white photograph suggested that it should be presented to anyone who opened the locker. That pleasure was still to come, as was actually trying to get dressed in the various modes of attire required for the different events of the next six weeks before we passed into the Army Apprentices College proper.

The rest of the day was filled with documentation and a tour of the camp showing us everything from the kitchens where we were to become the future

Master Chefs of the British Army – or at least that's what we were told, though who could blame us for thinking that; at this stage in our so far fairly uneventful lives, it might well be a little optimistic to look that far ahead.

Life can only get better

That evening brought a different outlook on the next day, as we were shown how to be 'properly dressed' for the start of our Military Training Phase, and the technicalities of various forms of dress made it seem imperative that to be dressed ready for the 06.30 parade before breakfast would mean rising from the comfort of our uniform-covered beds at around 04.30, and that was without taking into consideration the cleaning jobs that were, unknown to us, about to be posted on the heavily pinned notice board.

The practice of pressing green denim trousers without 'tramlines' was an art in itself and the smell of the spray starch sticking to the iron and leaving the familiar white residue still brings back memories of the twilight ironing sessions that, by the time the last person in the room got to the iron, was long after *News at Ten* was under way.

By this time we were using an assortment of phraseology that you only realise is unique to your particular arm of the service when you return to civilian company, words such as 'block jobs' and 'NAAFI breaks' that, if mentioned among your peer group of your previous educational establishment, would mean nothing and be received with blank looks. But here if you were not on the same wavelength and speaking the same lingo, the end results would often be to upset the nice calm way in which you hoped that life would flow along, though that rarely happened anyway as far as I can remember.

No matter what part of the country you were from whether Geordie or Jock, Paddy or Scouse they were all there in exactly the same boat heading against the tide with a very small paddle. But camaraderie was showing its head, and if one of us had a problem, then the others would soon join forces to sort the problem out.

One thing that I soon realised as a raw recruit from the sticks of Devon is that all people have very different ideas on how to live their lives. Until now smoking had been a thing that had been done in secret behind the bike sheds at school and was strictly forbidden, but here we were, 15-years-old, and smoking was permitted in the correct places.

As a non-smoker, the thought of my colleague opening his eyes at first light and reaching for the familiar No. 6 packet and allowing the flint to ignite the fuel in his lighter in order to kick start his lungs ready for the day still seems obscene. And this is a familiar sight to see wherever in the world the British squaddie is deployed.

There were of course the usual good-hearted initiation ceremonies that in my opinion were just that, and while I realise that if taken too far then these high jinks can be dangerous, there was nothing to suggest that this was the case at these barracks.

It was purely a case of the more senior intakes showing the junior recruits what they can expect to be able to hand out when and if they reach that grade. The Senior Squad were renowned for arriving back from the town, which incidentally was out of bounds for us except on Saturdays (and even then we had to be back in before *Saturday Grandstand* had finished), and on their return, usually when us nigs were tucked up in bed expecting to be there until morning, tipping us out of bed cursing under our breaths. Still, it was good practice in bed making – as this was only part of the Senior Squad, the other half should be back in an hour to improve on the bed tipping performed by their predecessors.

The Senior Squad were the lads who at the end of the term, in this case Christmas, would take part in the parade that marked the fact that they had completed their training, and after a well-earned spot of leave each would take his place in the regular Army attached as a cook to a unit to which he might or might not have wanted to go.

The next morning after a night of somewhat disturbed slumber we eventually managed to get attired in the drab green uniform that would, I hoped, soon look better than it did on that first morning. But we got the impression from the Platoon Sergeant that we were certainly not candidates to be placed on sentry duty at one of the more prominent of the English military tourist sights in this great country of ours.

We were stood in what was a rather disorderly three ranks which the Junior Corporal had done his best to arrange us in, with very little success, before the tonsils of the huge Platoon Sergeant let rip in full force. The hairs on the back of one's neck stood to attention as the rest of the large group of totally incompetent recruits should apparently have done.

The roll was called and at about a third of the way through the alphabetically arranged list a lone 'soldier' showed himself in the doorway of the barrack room block; it seemed there was always the one, or so Sarge said, and who were we to disbelieve Him! This man eventually took his place in the ranks causing total mayhem, because until then we had all known where to stand. Now there was an extra and, well! 43 men do not equally divide into three ranks; over to you Sarge, we all thought.

The first lesson of the day was an eye-opener, and certainly blew out the cobwebs that had been carefully accrued over the last fifteen years of sitting at the hinged desks of the schools and colleges of Civvie Street. How to stand properly to attention? 'Easy!' I hear you say! Yes, I thought so as well, but those of you who have spent any time in a military establishment will be well aware that, while the recipient of the lesson thinks he is doing it right, the Drill Instructor has his own very clear ideas and soon ensures that the basic recruit agrees with him, even down to trying bribery by offering a little stay in the 'Hotel' at the corner of camp, which to the well-informed was the jail – this was a good incentive to getting it right. We had seen the offenders being 'bounced' all around the camp at the speed of sound with laceless boots and witnessed them polishing to a highly mirrored finish the large brass bell that stood to the left of the door that led into the Provo Sergeant's domain. This was not for me if I could help it.

I can remember the faces pushed up against the

bars of the guardroom asking for a fag as the rest of life went on around them in the camp. We knew that if you were caught handing anything through the bars it would be a case of joining them on their daily round of litter clearing and polishing the already sparkling brass that adorned the camp. Fortunately, I didn't smoke so I could not have helped them if I had wanted to.

The first drill lesson ended at 10.10 and I would presume that had we got it right we would have had a chance of getting near the front of the NAAFI queue. As it was we might just have had the time to scoff down a tuna and cucumber roll and Coke, which should ensure we ended up with chronic indigestion to start the next session of the morning – PT, groan!!! Even to this day I am convinced that these sessions were paramount in persuading my subconscious that this was just torture and was never worth it; there were of course the few who had played various sports at levels that the majority of us only dream about, and they excelled in this area of activity.

A week went past and things got a little easier to understand though not easier to tolerate. Pay day made life a little more acceptable, although £1.50 did not seem to go far when you were expected to buy Blanco, boot polish and dusters, and any other luxuries such as chocolate came a very poor second.

The nightly queue for the two telephones seemed to get longer, and at the end of the first term the bill for the reverse charge calls made home would have paid for my own personal kiosk. But I found this was a necessary part of 'learning to deal with life'; whenever asked if I was enjoying it I always responded with a positive answer, and indeed I wouldn't have missed it for the world, even though at the time it would not have taken a great deal to make me throw in the towel.

Training progressed day by day and was supervised by a number of different instructors each, as you would expect, an expert in his own field. They certainly knew their stuff and now that I look back I realise just how good they were at getting the lesson across, especially when it boils down to the fact that the bunch of newly recruited civilians, apart from those that attended Army Cadet Forces (and I was not one of those), knew virtually nothing about the Army way of life or activities.

By the third or fourth week we could actually see an improvement in the standard of drill and the PT seemed to be getting easier, although the waiting room in the Medical Centre always seemed to be overflowing with soldiers doing their best to 'skive off' the morning drill parade or PT session.

There was an easier way to make the daily morning parade seem more tolerable, as will become apparent later.

We had now become a team and had started to get to know each other fairly well. The routine had fallen into place. The task of making 'bed blocks' was always a daunting one. For those of you reading this who are unfamiliar with bed blocks, this was a style of bed making where you stripped your beds and formed the three blankets and two sheets into a box shape, and this lay on the bed in front of the pillows and had to be of specific measurements or the owner would, on return from the drill square after the daily inspection of rooms had taken place, find his bed block torn apart ready for the task of the rebuild.

These bed blocks had to stay intact until the end of the working day, usually around five o'clock depending on just how well the Squad had performed on whatever the training task had been.

We soon found that one could not rely on the fact that, because tea was at 17.00, we would be finished by then, because the instructor would merely phone the kitchen and tell his fellow instructor that however many of us there were would want a late meal, and then there was that another hour of boot stamping or magazine loading before we could eat.

The evenings were taken up with the more traditional of pastimes that one naturally associates with the Army of that time such as 'bulling' boots to a high gloss ready for the next morning's parade. The expected standard was such that I very rarely reached it, and I was not the only one, but as time progressed so did the mirror-like shine on the leather toe caps of the 'ammo boot', an ankle-high, blister-making boot with leather soles. If you had been in any length of time they were adorned with large steel studs, and this soon became the early warning signs that the Platoon Sergeant was about to pounce on your room, because you could hear him coming from twenty paces. Thank goodness for tiled floors, you would think, but that took up the other portion of the evening! The dreaded task of polishing the floor so that your face could be seen in it was a nightly chore.

Tuesday evening had been aptly named as 'Bull Night'; this was the night prior to the Commanding Officer's weekly inspection, and the standard of the rooms was expected to be nothing less than 'as new' if not better. For those of you who have never heard of the term 'to bump' the floors I will do my best to explain. It derives from the piece of equipment that was used on the black tiled floors that were in this particular barracks at that time. The 'bumper' was a piece of iron about twelve inches long and four inches wide with a felt pad on the bottom, and protruding from this was a broom handle on a pivot. This was then run over the floor that had been layered with polish and allowed to dry. The implement hit the walls either end of the room with a loud bump; this is obviously how the name 'bumper' originated.

There was a certain fear instilled into us squaddies that if the rooms were not up to scratch there would simply be a reinspection the following day, which would mean another evening of burning the midnight oil getting it right.

Once we had completed the room to what we considered the correct standard we would sacrifice the use of blankets on our beds and transfer them to the floor so as not to scuff the polish before the dreaded inspection next morning. This done we would then send a 'spy' to see how the next room was looking and if they were better then up would come the blankets and down would go more polish. It was nothing to see two of the occupants of the room on their knees with a tin of Kiwi black boot polish and a duster, because this was one of the best products to produce the deep shine that was being hunted for by the whole of the college on the night before inspection.

When the Kiwi was dry another favourite to get the shine up was to put a roommate in a blanket, while another two would hold either end of the blanket and swing him up and down the floor. Windows were polished, chair legs Brassoed and locker tops dusted because as every soldier knew, the entourage that followed the Inspecting Officer ensured that if the first in line missed a speck of dust or a smear on the window the next would find it, and so on.

Of course there were not only the rooms to bring up to the level that was required, but each soldier on each floor of the three-level accommodation block had his own job to perform, cleaning the communal areas such as the ablutions, baths and showers, or even on the outside litter patrol. All were part of the rigorous task of ensuring that you were not under the same pressure the following night.

As the weeks went on there were of course the ideas that saved a lot of time, and others that would cause more trouble than they were worth, although I did manage to save myself the problem of making a bed block each day because I contrived to obtain a spare sheet and with careful folding made it look like two sheets in the block, so that as I slept with only two sheets and a bedspread on my bed, I could strip the bed in the morning, throw the sheets in the locker and replace them with the bed block, in the true *Blue Peter* tradition of 'Here's one I made earlier.' This went on for the two years that I spent at the college.

Although there was the requirement to make these blocks daily whilst in the Junior intake, after this period they were only made for inspections, but this little time-saver proved to be a godsend to me anyway.

Inspections were to prove a real nightmare for the rest of my Army career as you could never be quite sure just what the Inspecting Officer would be looking for, whether it was your turnout or your room, your kitchen or your surrounding areas that were being inspected. The fear was always hanging over your head that someone would have left a fag end under a bed or that your heavy duty green knitted jumper had a piece of cotton hanging from the back. Any of these trivialities could mean a reinspection or a visit to the guardroom at 2200 hours for an inspection in 'best kit', either of which was dreaded by all of us. Of course, there were the rare occasions when you would actually get through an inspection without being 'picked up' for anything and this was always a good reason to go to the NAAFI and celebrate with a pint of Coke. Remember we were only 15 so unable to celebrate with some of the stronger beverages that were to pass our lips in later years.

The very first room inspection that was to grace the squads of the 43rd Intake, a name which we had now received and were gradually becoming proud of, was an early morning affair at 0700 hours, and at around 0657 the voice of the Platoon Sergeant was heard bellowing the immortal words, 'Stand by your beds.' We all stood rigidly to attention, knowing full well that any one of us could be the lucky winner of a surprise locker inspection, a thought that induced horror into the pumping veins and arteries of the most hardened of the Apprentices at St. Omer Barracks.

The fingers of the Inspecting Officer shot into the air only to come to land on the top of a locker which fortunately for the whole room had been dusted with the expert skill that had become evident over the past few days, causing very little to be alarmed at. A slight glance to the bed mat opposite mine on which stood the size nine boots of my roommate showed a feather, one that had obviously escaped from a pillow and had avoided capture better than Ronnie Biggs. The owner of the mat saw my eyes trying to tell him something was adrift and followed my glances to the space between his boots and deftly moved his right boot two inches to the right and covered the offensive article. Eyes blinked shut around the room in a silent sigh of relief as the Inspecting Officer and his entourage left the room and we were given the order to stand at ease.

We would know if the inspection had gone well by whether or not a notice appeared on the board in the passage with the words 'Reinspection tomorrow'. If this was not there on our return to the room at ten o'clock, then we could rest easy.

During the first week we were all given what was to become, in my case, an identity for the next 21 years, the Regimental Number. I remember my father quoting his even after thirty years – it was embedded into his memory, and he was always telling me that his last three numbers were 007 so you can imagine the surprise when I received the piece of paper with my number and the last four digits were 0070; if that's not coincidence, then I don't know what is. I did not know how I was going to remember an eight-digit number that you need to write every time you fill out a form in order to obtain even the basic things from the Army like wages. The scrap of paper that the number was first presented on would soon be tattered and creased with the times that it was extracted from my pocket, but surprisingly it soon became firmly lodged in the grey matter beneath my skull.

Any serviceman or woman for that matter will, I am sure, never forget the number that they were issued with in that first few days of basic training.

Pay days were a little strange to the plain-thinking civilian minds that we still had. The thought of marching up to a table, halting and stating name, rank and number to obtain the customary £1.50 was a little daunting but soon became the easiest thing in the world, and no one ever asked what happened to the rest of our pay and when we would get it. This became evident at the end of term when we were paid our 'credits', which was all the money that had accumulated over the 14 weeks that we had endured. Most of us had around £90.00. This of course was considered a fortune, and after all it only had to last us for the three weeks of the Christmas leave period; but, although as I said we thought it was a fortune, all of us managed to spend the lot before returning to the barracks for our next instalment of training.

During the first six weeks of training we had to go through a selection of different routines and training lessons. The first lesson to ensure we were familiar with the effects of tear gas was an eye-opener. (Please excuse the pun.) We all stood there in the early morning with the dew still evident on the grass around the brick-built chamber that was going to reduce us to tears. The instructor pulled up in the by now familiar Land Rover and immediately gave orders to grab a suit from the back of the vehicle. We all clambered for the polythene-wrapped parcels that contained the NBC (Nuclear Chemical Biological) suits. Size, it appeared, was not important – as long as you had a suit which comprised trousers, jacket and hood, that was that.

For those of you who have never unwrapped one of these suits, they are vacuum sealed and if you are extremely lucky you may well be able to get the suit unwrapped and on your person within six or seven minutes; however, the stated time to adorn yourself in a real emergency is around the one minute mark with a swift nine seconds to 'mask up'.

Once in the suit the only thing that is required is the respirator or gas mask, and I can assure you that once you have a respirator on everyone takes on a new identity and that is one of 'all the same'; no one is recognisable, and it is only the piece of black tape with your name chalked on across your chest that separates the beautiful from the plain ugly.

As the instructor opens the door to the chamber and disappears into the eight-foot-by-eight-foot room your mind goes into overdrive trying to guess what comes next. Within minutes he emerges and removes his mask. It is evident that he has put the gas capsules into the chamber and lit them in order to give off the required fumes. He now begins to instruct on how we must act if our respirators should leak on entry: 'Don't panic, just raise your hand and point to the door where you will be let out to adjust your attire.'

Once inside and comfy we were told to report to the instructor one at a time and remove our respirators where we had to say our number, rank and name, before being allowed out in the reasonably fresh air that the Basingstoke Canal, which ran alongside the chamber, would give off at that time of the morning. Of course, the sadistic manner of the instructor seemed to make him deaf at the time when it was my turn to partake. I said what was required, and was just ready to turn and make for the door when the instructor said, 'I'm sorry, I didn't hear that – can you repeat it?' Well, for those of you who have never experienced the effects of tear gas, otherwise known as CS, it makes your eyes stream and your nose sting and various other nasty side effects take place. This was now happening, and I tried to repeat the answers that were required to effect my release from the evil-smelling gas, as I was becoming very uncomfortable. I finally managed it and was released into the morning air where various other members of the platoon were coughing and spluttering into the grass and trees that made up the training area. This made for a very interesting and different lesson and one that I did not want to repeat for a good long while and certainly did not want to be part of if it was for real.

That evening the talk was of how everything still smelt of CS and how we handled ourselves in the chamber, each claiming to have been subjected to worse than the other and how next time we would not be caught with our pants down, so to speak.

The first six weeks of training progressed, with the reward at the end being a long weekend at home.

Most of us had indulged in activities that we never knew existed until now, and one of the worst was PT. Some of the exercises that we had to endure seemed to put us into what I can only describe as a painful predicament. I remember one particular lesson where we had to place our backs against the wall and pretend to sit down with our thighs parallel to the ground and our arms folded in front and hold the position for 15 minutes. This apparently was a favourite exercise for skiers in order that they might strengthen their thigh muscles for their alpine escapades; if this is the case, then skiing is not for me. I shall stick to the easier sport of lifting a full pint beer glass and perfecting the distance between the lip of the glass and my own.

The Squad also took part in various runs and endurance tests; all these pursuits took place in different modes of dress, and by the end of the six weeks we were all getting the hang of the quick-change routine, almost to the stage where we could happily take part in the local theatre company's panto and change between scenes without assistance.

The favourite training area for endurance runs was around four miles from the barracks, and was where the testing for such war animals as the Chieftain tank were held. Obviously, this was a wet area even when the sun shone, and these great monsters had left huge grooves in the clay-coloured mud which, given the habits of the English weather, had soon filled with water.

One of the best games, as the instructors called them, was British Bulldogs, where two teams stood either side of the water-filled furrow and one team fought the other to reach the opposite side. This of course resulted in each and every one of us being drenched from head to foot in orangey grey water that we had to carry in our clothing back to our rooms.

As the sun started to rise on the sixth Thursday, we were rising from our beds in order to put the finishing touches to our brand-new uniforms that we had been painstakingly measured for three weeks earlier. Boots were bulled, brass polished, hair combed and eventually uniform donned in preparation for the 'passing in parade'. All our parents were invited and this was it; once we had completed this parade we were officially passed into the College Proper.

The Corps of Drums beat up a marching rhythm and the whole of the intake marched onto the square in three ranks, halting in the centre of the huge tarmac plain that the Regimental Sergeant Major considered to be consecrated ground. A smartly negotiated left turn saw us facing the crowd of parents, family and friends and at the same time feeling proud to have made it this far in our military careers.

The parade took about an hour and was completed by an inspection from an officer of very high status, whose name escapes me even to this day, but I do remember that even if it had been Royalty itself we, the Squad, could not have been better prepared. Day after day of practices and rehearsals had made us ready, although the bitter cold wind whistling across the drill square made the cold steel of our 7.62mm self-loading rifles almost impossible to keep a grip on.

The thought of dropping the weapon instils into your mind sheer fear and perhaps not just a little embarrassment, especially in front of so many people, two of whom just happened at that time to be the proudest people this side of the equator, or so they told me.

The parade came to an end and we had the opportunity to meet our parents and escort them to the wonderful lunch that had been laid on in their honour. It really stood for what Army Catering is all about. There may well be a lot of you reading these memoirs who have vivid memories of stew and dumplings and porridge and very little else, but I can now inform you that times have changed. To see a lunch meal in any of the military kitchens dotted around the globe makes the taste buds moisten, as your eyes meet with the six or seven choices that adorn the polished stainless steel hot cupboards with the infra-red heaters overhead.

After a hearty lunch we had the opportunity to give our friends and relatives the full guided tour of the barracks, and whether they found it interesting or not did not enter our minds! Of course, all we really wanted to do was head for home and the first long weekend's leave that we had worked so hard for over the last six weeks.

Everyone wore what is known as Number 2 Dress to go home, something which would be unheard of outside of the safety of the barrack gates these days, and of course that first weekend we were proud as peacocks, although on subsequent periods of leave nobody wanted to wear anything that resembled Army green, and when you are dressed in it seven days a week who can blame you?

I distinctly remember the last morning of leave; as I swung my legs out of the comfort of the quilt which, in a couple of hours, I would be deserting for another six weeks, I said to myself quite cheerfully, 'Oh Well!, back today,' and I suppose that at that stage I knew for sure that the Army was for me.

It was not until the train pulled into Aldershot and the Tower Block loomed into view that it became apparent that the first six weeks of what I considered to be hell was about to repeat itself, but in a more severe way than before, with the introduction of what we were there to learn, Catering.

Smart or what!

We took up a timetable of one week of Catering and one week of Military Training and Education, with subjects such as Catering Science and English. This was the format for the next two years, and it became easier as time went on. One of the first things that I remember cooking was fairy cakes – 'No rude remarks, please.' Considering that I had never touched a wooden spoon before this, and the mention of a roux conjured up the great Australian Outback with this huge creature bounding across the plains with a baby in its pouch, and not what the Chef Instructor was patiently trying to embed in our minds as the base for a sauce, I certainly had it all to learn.

As time went on we became more and more knowledgeable on culinary matters, although the kitchen was always the centre point for the dirty tricks brigade to be at their most active. Here we were, raw recruits with very little knowledge of what essences and flavours were available to us. So when the Instructor sent a young 15-year-old to the stores ten floors below for a bottle of 'white food colouring', he willingly accepted the task and started the long journey of eighty steps down to the bottom floor of the block. We knew something was afoot when the Instructor gave a snigger and lifted the phone that connected him to the stores in the basement and told the aged storeman that yet another gullible young recruit was on his way, to be kept waiting for what turned out to be a pint of milk. This, of course, was the only white colouring available and, on his return to the kitchen classroom he was greeted with the customary jeers. That soon became expected if you happened to be caught by one of the practical jokes that were tradition when a new boy came into any Army kitchen. It was nothing to be sent to the stores or some other place for a 'long weight' when in fact it should have been a long WAIT, and after the volunteer had been hanging around for a good twenty minutes or so he would be informed that he had his long wait and could now return to his place of work.

No matter where in the world you were posted, there would always be the practical joker in the kitchen, but that just went to make life that little bit more amusing.

As our training progressed so did our expertise, and different members of our intake excelled in different areas of what we were being taught. Earlier in these memoirs I mentioned a way to make the morning parade seem more enjoyable. Although I did not realise this was the case when I enrolled in the 'Corps of Drums' as a bugler and later to progress to the glockenspiel, I started to find these parades a lot easier than they previously were, and as I already had a musical background as a member of the local town band back in the more rural throws of Tiverton, where I had grown up, my introduction to the Corps of Drums was a little easier than it might otherwise have been.

One of the benefits of being a bandsman was that on morning parade the band was very rarely inspected, so that meant that you could get away with what you would have been jailed for in the normal parade format.

There were of course other benefits involved with being a member of the 'band', which involved trips to local fetes and displays, and as the Commanding Officer's Bugler I was required in November to play Last Post at the church on Remembrance Sunday. One year I was asked to play Last Post outside Windsor Castle for the local British Legion, which of course I consider a great honour to this day.

On the day that Her Royal Highness Princess

Anne wed Mark Phillips, four of the 'Corps of Drums', myself included, travelled to Threadneedle Street in London to the headquarters of the National Westminster Bank with our long fanfare trumpets to blow a fanfare for a Ladies' Dinner Night, a very proud moment for me and the rest of those involved.

Even the Sergeant Major marched to my tune!

There was a great deal of enjoyment in taking part in these events and my membership of the band lasted the whole two years that I was at St. Omer Barracks. Of course, there was the occasional heart-stopping moment when on the morning parade the Inspecting Officer decided to do a sharp left turn and head for the 'band', but I think that Lady Luck must have been looking down on us because, apart from the usual remarks of 'get your hair cut', we all escaped with our dignity still intact.

During the second half of the term we learned a great deal and friendships bloomed. Nicknames took the place of the handles that we had been christened with, and it became apparent that, if you had the slightest defect or unlucky break, it would not take long for someone to spot it and adorn you with your own. As I apparently at that time resembled the late and great comedian Harry Worth, I gained the name of Harry, and this is what I was hailed as throughout the training period. Even when I met members of my intake years later, I was still greeted as Harry. This can prove embarrassing.

There were of course the usual small groups that did their own things and went everywhere together, although in the first term as the junior intake these did not add up to much, and if the NAAFI was full then we would sit in our rooms and watch TV or listen to music.

Going to bed early was a risky thing to do because the dirty tricks brigade would be more than eager to use you as their guinea pig. I remember once I went to bed around nine, and, as many of you who have managed to sleep heavily for the first two hours will know, you can awaken abruptly thinking that it is morning when in fact it is only 11.00 pm. This is what they did to me. I was awakened by my roommate telling me that I had overslept, and they had excelled themselves this time. They had one guy getting dressed, one returning from the bathroom with a towel over his arm, another doing his room job; they had put all the clocks and watches forward, including my own. Well, I panicked getting dressed in a matter of minutes and heading for the ablutions for a wash and shave only to find, on return to my bedspace, four or five full sets of dentures smiling broadly at me from all the beds and *News at Ten* blaring nicely from the TV. Basically, I had been had, but all was taken in good part, and after all, I was as likely to be on the serving end of practical jokes as time went on.

As the term progressed, we started on the rehearsals for another parade, but this time we as an intake were not the starring attraction. It was the turn of the Senior Squad who had finished their time at the college and were about to take up, after a stint of leave, their posts throughout the world with whatever unit or regiment they happened to get, in what seemed like a raffle. The way it worked was that you put down on the relevant forms a choice of three areas that you thought you might like to be posted to. This was done at the beginning of the last term, and the results were announced just prior to the end of term. And, if your luck was in, the chances were that you would be posted within flying distance on a jumbo jet of your original choice of destination.

The Army has an uncanny knack of posting you to the opposite end of the country to that you originally requested, but of course there are the lucky ones who get just what they want. To be honest, this only happened to me once and I will cover this further on in these memoirs.

The cookery was progressing at a great rate of knots and we did appear to be learning a wide range of culinary skills, but of course we only made a very small dish of whatever was on the syllabus for that day, and this was very different from the 250 portions that I as an individual would be making in years to come.

When we had been marked on the performance for the morning's work, a representative for the class of twelve would collect all the food together on a trolley and transport it via the lift to the ground floor, where it was transformed into a huge mass to join the dishes prepared by the other classrooms in the Tower Block.

One of the best times for eating in the main dining room was when the soldiers who had returned for the advanced cookery course, known as the A1, were on their trade test week, and the culmination of three months' work came together and was tested by the Grade 1 Instructors. The choices were mouth-watering, and the dishes presented would have done justice to any of the world's top-class hotels or restaurants.

The soldiers involved were not only being tested for their Army qualifications but also for the City & Guilds of London Institute's certificate, something that has stood many an Army chef in good stead when he eventually moves from the vigorous routine of the Army to the even rougher world of the civilian caterer.

During the last term of the catering training there is a period in which the student is involved in 'bulk' catering in order to prepare for what he, or indeed she, can expect when posted to his first unit in the domain outside the confines of the training centre.

I witnessed many amusing incidents during my period in what is known at the School as K2 – this was the main kitchen for Apprentices, whereas K1 was the haunt for the soldiers who had enlisted at the age of 18 or older.

It was my squad's turn for breakfast this particular morning, and we were sharing the duty with another squad. The doors were unlocked at 0400 hours or for the civilian types reading this four o'clock in the morning. This rapidly became known as 'sparrow's fart' because nature has that peculiar habit of making the average person deposit all the air he has gasped in overnight and, as sparrows are always singing the dawn chorus before us, it obviously follows that the nickname stands to reason.

One particular soldier was sent to the large walk-in refrigerator to fetch the milk to complete the cereal bar. As in many large catering establishments, the milk came in the old churns holding many gallons of milk, and obviously these were very heavy. So, instead of calling for help, he decided to turn the churn on its side and roll it to the hot plate. This immediately caused the lid of the churn to be released and a white blanket was produced across the whole area of the kitchen. After the Shift Sergeant had contacted the air traffic control centre, he eventually came back down to earth and gave his vocal cords the airing they so obviously deserved.

Still, not to be outdone by this display of pure genius, another soldier was carrying a tray of potatoes to the oven. The tray measured in the region of three foot by three foot by one-inch deep and, on being confronted by a closed eye level oven door, he was, to put it mildly, confused where he would put the tray whilst he opened the door. As though he had been doing it all his life, he proceeded to toss the tray in the air, hoping to get the oven door open before the tray once again descended into his arms. The result was having to spend the next 20 minutes or so in retrieving potatoes from every spare nook and cranny in the kitchen.

There is for me, having been in Services, no better way to have obtained your experience. The variety and extremes that the Army chef has to overcome are second to none, from cooking in old tin cans to cooking sausage and mash for three thousand young lads on a Boys' Brigade rally.

Looking back, all these problems were tackled with vigour and enjoyment, and are certainly something that I will never ever forget.

CHAPTER 2

Leave was looming fast, the first long period of leave and, as the college was run along the same lines as a school, we used to have three weeks for Christmas and Easter and four weeks for summer. This was obviously the best thing that the year brought as far as the youngsters lining up on the parade square were concerned, for they knew that in less than three hours they would be scrambling for the limited number of minicabs that were available to transport the young soldiers to Aldershot railway station. That was, of course, provided the parade went well and, to be quite honest, the big ones always did. To give credit to the Drill Instructors, the rehearsals were always ropey but come the big day it was perfection in motion.

The sound of the leather-soled boots of over a hundred uniformed soldiers all hitting the ground simultaneously is one that, when you are part of a parade, brings a silent sigh of relief, because it only takes one individual to be a split second behind the rest and it stands out like a missing chime from Big Ben, and you know that the large-chested Sergeant

Major standing in front of the whole parade is going to be coming down on that individual very soon. And, of course that will, without a doubt, have taken some of the pride and pleasure out of the parade for all of you.

Fortunately this, as I said, was not the case for this first parade in which we had been involved since passing in to the college. The three weeks of leave that followed were very enjoyable, and that was aided by the fact that because we were only paid £1.50 a week over the last 14 weeks, we had without our real knowledge accumulated a good deal of credits, and while I realise that the sum that we received was not a great deal, £80 seemed a grand sum to us youngsters.

Of course, as time went on the amount at each leave period grew and grew until we were in the Senior Squad and receiving around the £200 mark.

There was the general bit of showing off, going to visit the relatives in full dress uniform when really after 14 weeks of wearing the same thing day in day out you could have killed for a pair of Levi's or the like. Still Mother had her ideas and to be honest I did not really mind because it still put a good feeling into your blood when your relatives and friends oohed! and ahhed! at you.

One of the things that was always the problem with leave periods was the amount of time you were given, because although we as a college were working along the same lines as schools, the holiday was never long enough. Still, I suppose ten weeks paid holiday a year was not bad.

Leave being finished, I made the long journey back to the home of the British Army, Aldershot, a trip that, by the end of the two and a half years, I came to detest. It seemed to last for ever and the very fact that the end of the journey did not exactly bring what we would have described as happiness made it worse. Although there were often enjoyable times, it did seem as though we would never end our training. I suppose it is on a parallel with school; when we were there it was hated by the majority of people, and the thing that really made me mad was the older generation telling me that it was the best years of my life. I could not bring myself to agree – that is until now, when all of a sudden I find myself sitting my own daughter on my knee and telling her exactly the same story.

That night, back at the college, there was all the usual banter of who had done what and who had been where. This of course was entwined with the laborious task of pressing kit and bulling boots. Some of the keener members of the platoon had done theirs before leaving home, but then there were always the ones who were aptly described as 'lickers' or 'grovellers' and showed distinct pleasure in being the first to do a particular task or job. Of course, these were the first to become Junior Non-Commissioned Officers, who were recognised from the rest of the motley crew by being adorned with a red and black chevron on the right arm just four fingers width from the edge of the shoulder.

For those of you who are wondering, the lowest grade were Apprentices, and so it went up from

Junior Lance Corporal to the top of the tree, Junior Regimental Sergeant Major, and there was only one of them, so you really had to be the bee's knees to attain that position.

I can hear you saying, or at the very least wondering, what rank I reached on this magnificent Junior scale. Well, to put you out of your misery, I was at one time on the very bottom rung of the ladder as an Apprentice. Perhaps I am leading you astray by not telling you that the time I was on the bottom rung lasted two and a half years, but at least I knew where I was and I can tell you that the lecture received on our initial arrival telling us that we were all future Master Chefs just seemed that little bit out of our reach.

The very fact that my friends were being made up (the phraseology for promotion) around me did not make that much difference to the friendship that had been built up between the now newly promoted Junior Non-Commissioned Officers and the rock-steady Apprentices like myself. I have a feeling that, at the time, the stories of it not making a difference to your career after leaving the college if you made it to Junior Sergeant or for that matter Lance Corporal were not entirely true, and if they were meant to make us feel better, then one has to say that they failed miserably. Still, I was enjoying life and I guess really that is all that really mattered.

Of course, to find out whether or not it did make a difference to my career I am afraid you will have to continue reading these memoirs to discover for yourself.

As the terms passed we had different activities to keep us occupied both day and night, and the usual exercises to remote parts of the British Isles were always greeted with delight (or nearly always). The Summer Camp was a fortnight in the beautiful gorse-and-heather-covered hills and tors of Dartmoor. The camp was situated at the top of a rather steep hill some three miles or so above the market town of Okehampton. The walk up from the town will I am sure have left a very strong impression on the minds of many an ex-service man or woman. Climbing the long drag whilst you were sober was one thing, but after a couple of pints of the local scrumpy, well, that was a completely different kettle of fish.

The Summer Camp started with a train journey from Aldershot to Exeter St. David's Station, which, as I am sure you will remember, is where my career had started more or less one year before, and the journey was completed with a coach ride through small Dartmoor villages such as Moretonhampstead and Princetown, home of the famous Dartmoor Prison, passing on the way other favoured landmarks of the area such as Postbridge and Haytor.

The arrival at Okehampton was no different from any other, and we all paraded to have our heads filled with the rules that now governed us for our two weeks stay in this wooden-hutted camp. It seemed to resemble the same sort of camp that was depicted in the TV series *It Ain't Half Hot, Mum*, except of course it was bloody freezing! Never let it

51

be said that in the midsummer months Dartmoor is hot!

The metal tubular steel bunk beds that went from the door to the distant end wall in perfectly parallel lines each had a mattress and pillow with two very worn discoloured blankets and two off-colour white sheets. If this had been a hotel, there would definitely have been grounds for the place to have been auditioned for *Fawlty Towers*, or at the very least shut down. Still, it did make our permanent homes at Aldershot look really good, and after all it was only for fourteen nights. I suppose that, looking back, it was not as bad as some of the places that I was to sleep in the twenty-odd years that followed.

I have slept in just about everything from the back of a four-ton truck to an old disused pillbox on the island of Alderney in the Channel Islands. But more about that later.

As the Summer Camp progressed there were of course all the things that were thrown into the programme to help us develop into the fighting chefs of tomorrow. The worst of all was the cross-country trek. Loaded up with a back full of kit weighing anything up to 25 lbs and a lump of gun metal in the shape of a self-loading rifle with a 7.62 velocity under our arms, we made a forced march of around 18 miles with all the usual map reading and survival skills being incorporated along the way.

Halfway through there was a rallying point to pick up one of the by now famous 'packed meals' which was sustenance for the second part of the trek. Now, whether it was pure coincidence or a premonition I don't know, but I distinctly remember saying to one of the lads in my group that I hoped there was enough for everyone, especially as we were the last group to see the checkpoint on the top of the next hill. This was probably due to a faulty compass; well, there was certainly no one in our group who was willing to take the responsibility at that particular point in time.

On arrival at the top of the huge hill, or tor in this case, our worst fears were realised – the packed meals had all gone, so as future trained soldiers we did the decent thing and carried on regardless, probably a foolish thing but at the time we did not think that.

Further into the day saw a distinct change in the temperature and the wind was definitely getting stronger. I remember we were walking in a straight line up a fair incline with the gorse and heather at knee height and the wind blowing in our faces when one of my mates went down on the ground face first and, thinking he had just tripped, I went to help him up, but he did not move. He had collapsed from the cold and no food.

The main problem was that with the wind blowing in our faces I could not make myself heard to the ones who were by now getting further away. I felt myself getting slightly panicky and my only hope was that one of them would turn around and see that I was in trouble. By this time my colleague had come around and was talking, so it was now vital that I kept him talking, and while that was happening the rest of the group realised something was wrong and came back to us.

After what seemed like an age, we arrived at the next checkpoint and explained what had happened. To our pleasure we were transported by Land Rover back to camp, and a lovely warm shower and hot meal.

After the initial week of the usual military-type games there was a week of activities and this gave me the opportunity to try dinghy sailing, something that before this camp I had never experienced. I knew that I was very prone to sea sickness so I was, to say the least, rather nervous, but I was pleasantly surprised because, I presume, the fact that I had work to do on board (to use the correct Naval phraseology) acted to relieve my mind from the nausea created by the swell. The stretch of water was situated off the Citadel in Plymouth, and the fact that I was now sailing in the same place from which Sir Francis Drake spotted the Spanish Armada was for me a great thrill. It only goes to show that the old adage of 'Join the Army and see the world' is very true. I can quite honestly say that if I had not taken heed of this advertisement then I would be without 95% of the things that I have done in my 36 years so far.

Returning to St. Omer Barracks in Aldershot created mixed feelings, but certainly brought a good night's sleep, which everyone needed after a very rigorous fortnight on Dartmoor.

My return from the bleak, orange and yellow

heather-carpeted expanse of these Devon moors showed that I had become victim to a torn cartilage in my left knee, and this was causing me a great deal of pain and discomfort, especially when my knee locked and the pain psychologically disallowed me to straighten out my leg, and this then of course had to be done by someone who was near the scene.

I was admitted into the Cambridge Military Hospital and underwent the operation to remove the cartilage from my affected knee, and on awaking from the anaesthetic I found I was adorned with a huge pressure bandage, as this was in the days before microsurgery. A good seven days laid up in bed and the opportunity to make new friends caused us to enjoy our stay rather than make it an ordeal.

Most of the patients in our ward had undergone operations similar to mine or related to the limbs in some way or another, and it was that time of the day when the Matron of the hospital was about to enter the ward on her weekly inspection. One of the most regular questions asked on this particular ward was 'Have you been doing your exercises?', which for myself consisted of lifting the leg four inches or so from the bed, holding for a couple of seconds and lowering. This would once again build up the muscles of the leg and reduce the need for long term physiotherapy.

The Matron, a middle-aged Lieutenant Colonel, entered the ward and proceeded to lift the small record boards from the beds and ask the patients the aforementioned question. I replied that yes, I had, so she proceeded to the next bed and before lifting the board asked the occupant, 'Have you been doing your exercises?' with which the whole ward erupted into laughter, which for some of us caused more pain than the pre-med injection. The Matron did look baffled, and it took the Ward Sister to whisper in her ear that the soldier involved had undergone a circumcision to make the Matron realise what all the fuss was about. The inspection ended at that very bed and left the 15 or so patients with a really good story to tell on return to their mates.

I was lucky enough not to need a course of 'physio' and on return to my unit I had to really go in order to avoid being put back one term or, in our language, 'back squadded'. Thankfully this was not the case, and I went on with my training after a spot of sick leave, which was certainly a bonus and, because I had spent the best part of the term in hospital I had accumulated a lot more 'credits' than anyone else.

Leave periods came and went, and for each one that passed I left more and more Army kit behind and only took the required civvies home with me.

The final term started with a new Senior Squad, with R, S, T and U Squads forming that body of men, and we were going to be the toughest Senior Squad since the barracks opened. I suppose that everyone thought that when they reached the pinnacle of their training, and we were certainly no exception.

Before we finished that final term of service, we had to undergo what had now firmly earned the name of Battle Camp, which was to take place in the

Channel Islands on the Island of Alderney. For those of you who have never been to this beautiful little island, it really is just that. We left the military port of Marchwood just across the water from Southampton for the nine-hour crossing to the island.

I am not the best traveller and within minutes I was precariously hanging over the side rail and depositing yet more pollution into the English Channel. This lasted for the whole nine hours and was, I thought, the worst feeling in the world. There is just no escape, and I thought 'never again', but worse was still to come, as you will discover later in these memoirs.

We arrived at Alderney and all dispersed from the boat with a week ahead of us. That evening was spent settling in and, for me, getting over the nauseating journey across the water. The best thing I remember is the price of the drinks in the pubs; if I remember correctly, it only cost us ten pence for a short. We participated in various exercises and spent one night in a Second World War bunker, which was extremely cold, and as the flames flickered from the small cube of hexamine, it seemed as though the mess tin perched on the top of the disposable stove would never be hot enough to add the instant apple flakes that were to make up my sweet for that evening. The mess tin would have to be rebuilt for the coffee or tea or for that matter anything else that you required to eat or drink, and because all this took so long most people ate the 'compo' rations cold. This was quite feasible as they were designed to be eaten either way. The small box known as a '24-hour rat pack' contained a specially balanced meal for one man to last one day and contained most things that the average soldier would need including a tin opener and around six sheets of rather harsh toilet paper, something that I am afraid I never used, and it did not take long before one of the first things that got packed into my large pack was a lovely soft toilet roll.

We were due to pass out from the college in the December of 1973 but a few of us had entered for the Salon De Culinaire de Londres, or 'Hotelympia' as it is better known amongst the catering fraternity, and we had to return after a wonderful Christmas break to practise and complete our final pieces for entry on the crucial day in order for them to be judged. I remember vividly waiting outside the hall in which we had our pieces displayed for the judges to make their final decisions.

Finally, the doors opened and the writhing mass of entrants flooded in. From then on there was the usual chorus of jubilation and sadness.

I had entered an exhibit in the works in the 'potato' class, and had manufactured a cannon by weaving around sticks with a specially prepared potato peeling and then deep frying until crisp. The 'dangerous' part is when the sticks are removed, as this is the time when the potato either breaks or comes off in one piece, and I can tell you that twenty-one attempts before finally achieving the best end result I could ask for really is enough to give even the hardest chef in the world a nervous breakdown! All this hard labour resulted in me being awarded the Silver Medal; I was over the moon, and the most nerve-racking time was the four or five steps up to the stage to receive my medal.

Once this ceremony was over, I returned to Aldershot with all the other medal winners and prepared myself for my first posting as a fully qualified chef with my City and Guilds 706/1.

How's this for a spud gun?

CHAPTER 3

The train left Aldershot station and I watched the telegraph poles slip by the window. I must have fallen asleep because before I knew where I was we were pulling into Chippenham station in Wiltshire. As I handed in my ticket to the uniformed guard at the little box on the side of the exit from the platform, I looked around for my chauffeur-driven limousine. Ah, there it was; in the familiar mottled green colours of my camouflaged jacket it looked like a convertible – the Land Rover they had sent could have the roof removed in hot climates.

The drive from the station to my new home, Basil Hill Barracks in Corsham, was about three miles, to a reasonably small cluster of buildings all built from Bath stone and blending in well with the rest of the surrounding area.

I was dropped off at the guardroom, and it must have been habit that made me introduce myself as Apprentice Rowcliffe; it had not really registered that I was now a Private.

With that introduction over, I was shown to my room and was pleasantly surprised to find that for the moment anyway I was not sharing with anyone; still, I was soon informed that another chef would soon be joining me. Oh well, never mind! All sorts of thoughts were rushing through my head as I unpacked and started to get myself together, when a figure I had not realised was there spoke from the doorway and informed me that I was required by the Master Chef in the main kitchen.

I was ushered into the Staff Sergeant's office and stood like a steel girder, rigid to attention, and was told to take a seat. Was this a ruse to catch me unawares? – or perhaps this is how the real Army works. I took him up on his offer but declined the cup of tea that to look at would have been better carved with a knife than poured from a pot; still, the thought was there.

I was given a short talk on how HIS kitchen worked and how he expected me to work, and all in all it seemed to be a most likeable place. Before very long I was being introduced to the rest of the staff, at least those who were on duty at that time, and being told, 'See you at 0830 in whites, ready to start the day.'

Well, at least I had the evening to settle in and the best place to do this according to my new colleagues was in the bar.

There were of course all the usual stories told in order to scare the living daylights out of me; advice to 'stay away from him, but he's OK' went in one ear and out of the other; still, I suppose they were only trying to help. It did not take long to make new friends and this was the case wherever I went. I always found that part fairly easy and I think I can say without too much doubt that I did not make any real enemies, with the exception of course of Saddam Hussein.

Tuesday morning saw the dawn rise over the Wiltshire hills, and the ringing in my ear told me that it was time to throw back the covers and approach the day with as much eagerness as I could possibly muster. I washed, shaved and adorned myself in the immaculately pressed whites and walked towards the kitchen quivering with what was to be my first experience of being an Army Chef Proper.

As I entered the kitchen there was an eerie silence and I thought that this was not the Army kitchen that I had come to know and love from my two weeks in 'bulk' at K2. There was an elderly gentleman at the huge washing-up sink who, from the look of him, had been there since time began, and oblivious to me he was singing a chorus from Frank Sinatra's 'My Way'; this and many other 'hits' became the focal point of the whole kitchen.

I asked in what must have been a very nervous voice where everyone was and I was pointed in the direction of a small room where, sat around a small table, were various people in different states of dress. As I entered the room a silence fell, and as I was very nervous I was not going to be the one to break it. But I need not have worried; someone, I can't remember who, said, 'Get yourself a cuppa.' This was never the case at Aldershot; when you entered the kitchen then you started work at once, but here! well, if you had not had a cuppa how could you possibly be expected to work to the best of your abilities?

The time was now 8.30 and no one was making a move to start work when all of a sudden the civilian gentleman I had met earlier entered the room and said the boss was on his way. Well! never let it be said that the chefs of the British Army cannot move fast because before I could raise my cup for the next sip of coffee the room was empty and I was left to myself.

The boss, a rapidly ageing gentleman and obviously about to finish his 22 years, entered the kitchen with a certain flair and I could not help but notice that, as he made his way through the maze of stainless steel tables that made the main area of the kitchen shine like a mirror, his eyes were everywhere, and he did not let one thing go unnoticed. This technique, I thought, had taken a great many years to acquire, but he managed, in a matter of around 30 seconds, to have the complete shift buzzing to clean up or put right what should have been done before the first cup of tea had even brewed.

The comments about the amount he had drunk the night before went around the kitchen silently but effectively without the gent in question even knowing it, until a voice boomed from the office, 'And I wasn't pissed last night.' This man really was good; he had an astonishing ability to control and dominate people without even leaving his office. I vowed that one of these days I would be like him!

I did not know what to expect when I was

summoned to this superbeing's office at around nine o'clock and told to sit down. A new side to the boss was now being revealed, one that I had not seen before, the warm human side – that of a father figure really. But what did he want in return? I asked under my breath. That soon became evident as he handed me a polythene-covered piece of paper with the heading DUTY COOK'S DETAIL. This meant the worst, that I was Duty Cook tonight. I thought that this was it, the 'make or break' of my stay at Corsham, but then I was told not to worry, I would not be alone. I was to learn the ropes from one of the other more senior Private soldiers that the Master Chef had in his domain.

I was put to work with a rather plump but jolly sort of man who had been in many years and apparently knew everything there was to know about catering but had never risen any higher than the rank of Private. There were a number of these sort of people that I came across in my career and they were all basically the same as each other.

As the morning progressed the personalities of the kitchen became prominent and each had his own little way of behaving and taking life in his stride. As the hands on the clock progressed towards 10.00 the sound of a tray of cups and mugs being assembled only spelled one thing, that it was nearing teatime, and at bang on the hour the whole kitchen ground to a halt for NAAFI break. It was not until I had completed numerous years that I realised that if the Russians wanted to attack the British Isles then there were three good times to do it: No.1 was at ten in the morning, No.2 was on a Wednesday afternoon when the whole Army less the cooks were playing sports (the cooks were never very sporty) and No.3 was on a Friday afternoon when everyone, less the cooks again, had finished for the weekend.

It did not take long to realise that to be in with any sort of chance of getting a chair in the small emulsioned rest room you had to have all your work done and tables and work area cleaned before you even considered leaving the kitchen. Obviously this was something that I needed a lot of practice in, because the first week I barely managed to see the last five minutes of the 20-minute break, let alone take part in the card game that took place in the centre of the room. This is an activity that most chefs in the Army indulge in during the morning and afternoon tea breaks, and no matter where in the world the Army chefs are deployed there are always 52 pieces of cardboard with the various colours and numbers that go to make up the standard pack of cards.

It was, as I said, a good couple of months before I was even invited to play a hand. When I look back I realise that this was out of kindness, as I probably would have lost all my money, because although there was never any money on the table there was always a 'kitty' – which was, of course, to the Army's way of thinking completely illegal, although it still goes on all over the world.

When I did eventually get into the game I did exactly what was expected of me; I lost all my money!

It did not take an age to realise that if I only took a small amount with me to work then, if I did lose, I would only be a little out of pocket.

These tea breaks became a discussion group as to what everyone had done, or seen on TV, the previous night, and I would suppose that as with any working environment tea breaks never lasted long enough.

I soon got into the swing of the way that the kitchen worked and as a young newly qualified chef I seemed to be getting all the duff jobs including making the huge pot of gravy, or as it is known in military circles 'brown sauce'. As Duty Chef it was my job to make the six gallons or so that was required for the next day's consumption, and if it wasn't right then you were really for the high jump. I eventually landed the job of Pastry Cook for a week, which meant I had the making of all pastry and sweet products for the kitchen, and I feel I was fortunate; I now realise that it could have been worse as this was only a small kitchen.

Every day there was a requirement for eight pudding basins of steamed pudding, various cold sweets and quite a few crusty apple pies. The recipes are still completely embedded in my brain and will probably stay with me forever. I certainly learned a lot from my posting and it was just as with all other things – the training is only the beginning and you do not really start learning until you are 'out on the ground'.

It was becoming obvious that the majority of the kitchen hands were rather advanced in years, some more than others. In fact, there was one old fellow who probably knew more about this particular kitchen than the rest of the crew put together, but this was very common, as any Army cook will tell you. Even in Germany there was always one member of the kitchen staff who had been there since the War finished, and if the worst came to the worst then this lady or gent could always be relied on to provide information on what happened last time. Of course, you did not let on to the Master Chef that old Harry told you to do it that way or your life would not be worth living.

I had only been at this unit around six months when I purchased my first car. It was a 1965 Morris 1000 and I was as proud as punch of this wreck, which, now I look back, was all it was. Still, it was mine and it was paid for. Of course if you had a car you were always handy for a lift to the pub or for some other business that warranted the use of a vehicle of some kind, and it was for this reason that the boss called me into his office one day and said, 'Sit down.' Ah! I thought, here we go.

I am sure that I have said this before, but when the boss calls you into his office there is either something wrong or he requires you to volunteer for something, and as it happens in this case it was the latter. 'I would like you to do me a favour.' When I asked what the favour was, 'Sunday' came the reply. I offered my apologies and told him that I was working that weekend. This was when the unheard-of happened. He told me there was no need to worry; he would fix that if I helped him out. I felt myself getting drawn into a hole that, before very much longer, I would be unable to climb out of. 'OK,' I said, 'what is it that you want me to do?'

This was when I started to feel like a member of a secret organisation because it transpired that this gent had left his wife for another lady and had taken several small items of the matrimonial home with him. This is where the problems arose. His wife was now coming back to him, but the treasured items in question were still with his girlfriend and he had to get them back before Monday.

So, after a good thirty seconds hard thinking about a weekend to my credit, I agreed to take him to the girl's home to pick up the picture that had been left there. You will notice that I did not say house, and the reason is that when we arrived at the place in question it was a caravan park.

We were invited in for lunch and I sat at the table opposite a very attractive slim lady who really was quite stunning, and as I looked the room over I noticed that on the shelf behind this lady was a photograph of the very same female dressed in exactly what the good Lord had adorned her with on the day she was born – NOTHING! This made the swallowing of the Brussels sprouts very difficult, especially as I had now realised that the caravan park was a nudist camp.

I sat through the rest of the meal and gradually disposed of the sweat that began to grow under my collar, and it really was a case of being glad to leave because, although we were made to feel very welcome, I can assure you that it is very difficult trying to get through a three-course meal with the hostess staring you in the face NAKED.

On return to my room I, of course, as a young red-blooded man, could not wait to tell the story and for a short while I was the envy of all my colleagues.

I soon became one of the Catering team, and it does not take one long to realise that no matter how experienced you are you are certainly only part of the team. The day that you are first Duty Cook, a duty for which everyone forms a hatred, is one that sends shivers up your spine. There you are alone in this huge kitchen and in a position of responsibility; if anything happens now there is only yourself to sort it out.

There were, of course, always the problems of late meals, or the guardroom not having any milk, and many other little trials and tribulations that were sent to bug the young Private.

It soon became obvious to me that there was a particular brand or breed of Duty Cook who was convinced that he could pull the wool over the eyes of the boss, and what is more he thought that he could get away with it. Early each morning the Master Chef would do his daily check on the previous evening's production, and this could include anything from a sack of Brussels sprouts neatly peeled, sized, and adorned with the small cross on the underside, to 50 steak and kidney pies all made from scratch. But the favourite thing to check was the 'brown sauce' or, as many who are reading this will know it, the gravy.

If there was anything that was going to be wrong,

it was always the gravy. Remember that this was before the days of the Army chef using instant gravy powder and other commercial brands that took away the need to stand over six gallons or more of the thick dark brown liquid that was poured over thousands of soldiers' meals at that time. The first question that always escaped from the lips of the boss was, 'Did you use cornflour?' and even though the shine that was given off in the early morning light was enough to tell this, the most intelligent man in the kitchen, that cornflour was used as a shortcut, the Duty Chef still denied it.

The punishment for most of the chefs who 'cocked up' on duty was extra duties, which were a godsend to the one whose duty was replaced, but a real nuisance to the chef taking the punishment. There was of course always the one on whom 'extras' did not have the slightest effect, and he or she ended up on 'orders', which is to say being put on a charge, or punishment list, and this indeed could affect your social life even more.

There was the time when I was working in the Sergeants' Mess and it was my responsibility to prepare the breakfast for the civilian waitress to serve to the mess members. This morning there was, it would seem, no real need to rise from the comfort of the crisp white cotton sheets that had become wrapped around my torso. If there had been, then I would have heard the alarm clock and been in on time. The fact that the waitress had done all the breakfasts gave her the opportunity to let me know that she only did it for people ONCE! I suppose I really had to try her out, and the following morning I repeated the previous morning's programme, and arrived at the mess to find the waitress propped against the table and numerous members of the mess standing in front of the raging gas grill and cooking toast like it was going out of fashion. I then heard the voice of the senior member very briefly telling me I was on a charge.

Even making sure that I arrived at the Q's door before the rumours reached him failed to save me from parading in front of the Officer Commanding's office door.

It was, and I believe still is, the custom for chefs to parade on disciplinary interviews without apron and hat, and that was my position now. I was soon to know the outcome of my visit, and if anything was a certainty it was that I would be less well off in around five minutes time.

I was marched into the large office with a huge antique mahogany desk sitting pretty on a large square oriental type rug. Sat behind it was the Major, a man of around forty and looking as though he could eat me for breakfast. I marked time for around twenty steps before the foghorn voice of the Sergeant Major ordered 'Halt!' and I stood, as so many others had done before and since, staring into mid-air and listening to the words of the charge being read by the C.O.

I about-turned and marched out of the office with seven days restrictions of privileges. This meant that it was the last time I would see my civilian attire for a week, and I had to report to the guardroom at

1800 hours for two hours' work and then back to the guardroom at 2200 in best kit for an inspection, and if you were found to have something wrong then you could expect to be back at 2300 and every hour through the night until you had it right. This may sound as though it is not much of a punishment, but I can assure you that to a young hot-blooded male who wants to be out drinking and generally having fun it is a real nuisance, and in many ways worse than a fine of £50.

As anyone who had been on orders arrived back in the kitchen the vultures would descend on him to find out just what form of punishment had befallen him.

But of course, the majority of people who have served in the Armed Forces will, at some time in their service, have been on a charge or in trouble for something; that happens all the time in service life. I remember one such occasion when my block job was to clean the bathrooms and sinks, and it was the day of an inspection. I always had a check over the tiled floor before I left for work, and this particular day all was well and the area was spotless, so I left for my place of employment with what I thought was a clear conscience. However, on my return that lunchtime, I found a note that said all was not well and I was to report to the Sergeant Major.

This I did, and was told that I had let the whole block down because a cigarette end had been found in the toilets! When you are in this position you soon get to realise that it does not do you any good to protest as you are on the losing side, and this is definitely a case of guilty until proven innocent rather than the reverse.

I thought that the fact that I did not smoke should have held some clout but not a bit of it. I was immediately warned in the proper way that I would be charged.

This meant that yet again I was paraded in front of the Commanding Officer and rewarded with a suitable punishment to fit the offence.

I suppose now that I look back on my life in the Army I realise that all these events go to make up and prepare a young man for the 'rich tapestry of life', and it certainly has done that for me. If I compare myself to my colleagues who attended the same school as me, then I have not missed out on much as far as the richness of life is concerned.

While I was at Corsham I soon made friends with one of the several chefs who, for reasons that I cannot remember, were ex-RAF cooks who had transferred to the Army. He rather took me under his wing, and I found that before very long I was becoming a part of his family and for a small spot of babysitting was able to enjoy a homely atmosphere that was unavailable in a room that sported only a bed and a wardrobe. This certainly made settling into a new environment much easier.

I was finding that life out of training bore no comparison to the harsh life at Aldershot. Because we were permanent staff, we had our own bar and social club, which, although managed by NAAFI, was an acceptable place to retire to in the evening to enjoy a pint of the amber nectar after a long hard day over a boiling hot stove. The only thing that could really put the mockers on the whole evening was the thought that because you had an early shift the next day it meant greeting the day with the birds at around 0530.

It was while I was on one of these shifts that the Corporal who was working with me decided that I should be able to get on with the breakfast while he did something that had needed doing for ages. Well, who was I to argue? He was the Corporal and I was the Private, so I continued to fill the air with the delicious aroma of the bacon sizzling nicely under the grill and turning the neatly cut slices of fried bread in the hot fat that filled the large fryer.

I turned to see the Corporal using the sharpener that adorned the top of the large electric bacon slicer. The blade spun round at a great rate, and I heard him announce that it should be sharp enough now and, before it had completely stopped rotating, he decided to rest the fleshy part of his thumb on the blade to see exactly how sharp it really was. The answer is that it was sharp enough to send blood pouring from his hand and drip continuously on the floor as he wandered around the kitchen in a state of shock. After several minutes I managed to get him to stand still long enough to get a clean cloth wrapped around the thumb and get him to the Medical Centre.

When he returned, breakfast was over and I received a very uncustomary pat on the back for carrying on and feeding the hungry hoards, who had queued at the door for a good twenty minutes before the meal was due to start.

Of course he did not even mention the thumb that by now was adorned with a thick clean white bandage and was obviously giving him a fair deal of discomfort, but I suppose that it did not seem to be the right thing to let his subordinates see that he had done a rather silly thing.

I never saw him touch the machine after that episode and it obviously did not do him that much harm because he went on to achieve higher things – the rank of Warrant Officer Class One. I have decided not to mention names in these memoirs because so many people helped to make the military life so varied and it is not, I believe, fair to single out any particular person, and besides the people who are described will recognise themselves, I am sure.

Before too long I was given my own room. Those of you who served in the Forces will realise this was normally only for those of, at the very least, Non-Commissioned Officer status, and for a Private who had not been out of training for a year it was very unusual. Still, it made my life a lot more comfortable and certainly improved my standard of living.

My time at Corsham was a very good learning experience, and one of the things that I especially remember was learning to make bread. The Corporal who taught me this skill was a very short Geordie with a nose that had obviously taken a battering in the boxing ring at some stage because it was, to say the least, misshaped.

The skill of breadmaking is an art, and those of you who have ever made bread will know that it never turns out like the favourite brands that appear on the supermarket shelves, but is a lot tastier, though for some reason it has the remarkable knack of giving you chronic indigestion if eaten warm; but then, if you liked freshly baked homemade bread you were prepared to suffer some discomfort.

One of the other important lessons that I learned on this first of many postings was that if trouble started brewing anywhere in the world then political pressure would mean that British troops would stand a more than average chance of being involved. This happened with the Cyprus crisis in 1974 and I was immediately transferred to an RAF station called South Cerney, which is the air trooping centre for the British Army and is where almost all troops who are travelling abroad report for documentation before moving on to their base airfield for take-off.

I was sent there for a week and was part of the team which was manning a 24-hour kitchen; breakfast started at midnight and finished at 1000 hours, lunch then started until three o'clock and then tea was served from three till midnight. I thought I was lucky to catch the night shift but how wrong I was! I helped to serve 2,000 men the first night and 15,500 the second; after that it did get a little quieter, but not much.

However, it was a good experience and one that stood me in good stead for the next 20 or so years, and even more so for the life in Civvy Street.

As life went on so did all the experience that you gain by working in an environment where something new happens every day, as it did in this and every other kitchen I ever worked in, and as days and weeks went by I continued to enjoy the life that the Army had to offer me.

By now I had equipped myself with a new motorcycle, a beautiful emerald green Italian-made Benelli with an engine capacity of 250 cc, this of course being the days before the restrictions for learner drivers and when petrol was costing me an average of 50p a gallon.

I used this mode of transport to convey myself on the two-hour journey from Corsham to Tiverton in Devon, and it is not hard to look back and realise that the young man's brain lets him take risks that the more mature man would not have taken. I was always trying to do the journey just that little bit quicker than the last time. I was lucky that I never came to any harm, as I now of course realise.

Being a man who has indulged in a few 'get rich quick' schemes (and I hasten to add, failed!) I was more than interested when my friend invited me to help him with the selling of items that he had purchased from a wholesaler and that he hoped he could sell from the back of his caravanette and make a quick profit. This was obviously illegal as far as the Army was concerned, and so as not to bring down the wrath of the gods he would spread the word at the hotplate as the soldiers came through for their meals, and inform them that his van would be parked outside the camp that evening and they would be welcome to come and view the merchandise at their leisure.

But of course, we were soon stopped from 'trading' as the customers ran out, but that did not seem to matter because we had made a few quid, which was what we set out to do.

For those of you who are reading these reminiscences and have not served in the Forces, it is very common for members to try and augment their pay packets with whatever form of employment they can find, after, of course, obtaining permission from their Commanding Officer. I myself have over the years been employed as a barman, a grill chef, and a taxi driver, to name just a few, but of course none of this affected the way the highly trained individual went about his normal day's work for his Queen and Country.

One of the things that I had never realised was just how fast time would pass in the Army. It felt like only a couple of weeks since I had been posted to the Bath stone buildings of the barracks in Corsham, and now clutched strongly in my hand was a piece of paper that told me I was about to embark on my first overseas posting. The order said that I was posted to the RHG/D, which of course did not mean an awful lot to me, but I was soon to find out that this was indeed a quite unique part of the Army and one with many traditions, and was otherwise known as the Blues or the Royals. This regiment was stationed in Detmold, West Germany, and I cannot quite explain to this day the feeling that you get when you receive a posting order to move you on to the next chapter in your life, especially if you manage to get promotion as well.

This was not to be in my case, but never mind, these were early days and I was now a lot more experienced in the way of life as an Army chef, or so I thought.

I reported to the Air Movement Centre in Hendon, London and was given a bed for the night, in order to be transported at first light to Luton Airport for the hour-and-a-half flight to RAF Gutosloh. This meant a coach ride of about an hour, on the wrong side of the road of course, and allowing for the usual delays and hiccups or, as they are aptly described in the Army, cock-ups, it was already getting dark as the continental-style coach drew up outside a rather grey and dull looking building, which would have been an ideal setting for a German prison. I disembarked from the coach and surveyed the ground before me and thought of the nice familiar surroundings that I had left only hours before; then, with a sharp intake of breath, I made my way to the large, ornate wrought-iron gates that blocked the only entrance into this camp, or Kaserne as the people of Detmold referred to it.

I was approached by a soldier wearing a khaki greatcoat – incidentally no longer issued, but when they were they proved a great blessing, as they did manage to keep out the cold. The man was armed with the usual weapon, a self-loading rifle with a 7.62 calibre, and I reached for my identity card and produced the evidence that the guard needed in order to admit me into the home of the Household Cavalry, or at least part of it.

My first impression of the camp was that the very old buildings were all centred around the hallowed ground, otherwise known as the drill square, and as I entered the guardroom I realised that this was indeed one of the more traditional of the old Army regiments. As I have already said, it was known as the Blues and Royals, but they were more formally recognised as the Royal Horse Guards and Dragoons or RHG/D.

I was greeted by a gentleman of around 35 years old to whom I gave my rank and name, and told him that I was posted to the unit. After numerous phone calls to various anonymous voices at the other end of the line, he nodded and replaced the receiver, and hinted that I should follow him.

On his right arm were three stripes and a crown, so I knew very well that the correct address for him was 'Staff', especially as he was adorned with the insignia of a Staff Sergeant or so I thought. However, as you would expect, in the Household Cavalry they liked to be that little bit different, and the striding Non-Commissioned Officer that I was trying to keep up with was only equivalent to a Corporal, but he was called Lance Corporal of the Horse! Well, I ask you! It turned out that if the NCO had two stripes and a crown he was a Lance Corporal; three stripes and a cloth crown was a Corporal. Three stripes and a brass crown was Corporal of Horse and therefore equivalent to a Sergeant. Easy really, and certainly by the end of a three-year posting it became firmly embedded in my brain.

It was a tradition which, according to the regiment's older generation, stemmed back to the days of Queen Victoria when the Household Cavalry were the Sovereign's own regiment, and as 'sergeant' roughly translated means 'servant', the Queen wanted to show that her soldiers were not servants, so they were given these rather different titles. This went right up to the top of the Non-Commissioned ladder where the Regimental Sergeant Major became the Regimental Corporal Major.

As the time of my arrival was quite late I was shown to a room where, when I opened the door, the occupants were obviously in a hurry to leave the barracks and prop up the bars of the local watering hole, which incidentally could be seen quite clearly straight across the road, and bore the quaint German name of 'Henry's'.

No matter where in the Federal Republic you happened to be posted, it seemed that the pubs were not called by the names on the ornately painted signs hanging outside the premises, but by the name of the landlord, and this made identification even easier.

Detmold had its fair share of drinking establishments and I must admit to you I frequented a fair few of them, but the names are just memories. I wonder if those of you who were ever posted to this lovely German market town remember the Half Way House, and Gunters. These were only the German pubs; there was also the Rose Bowl on the large concrete jungle of Hakadahl, the British soldiers' married quarters estate. This was a sort of social club for married couples who lived on the estate and did not want to visit the local German establishments, and was certainly a favourite haunt on a Sunday lunchtime.

Compared with the small estate that I lived on in Corsham this one was massive, and the small green wooden hut which served as the family shop in Corsham was a different ball game from Detmold, which had at the time one of the biggest NAAFI establishments in West Germany. With such a good selection the British soldier did not need to visit the local shops, and of course there were those who rarely did, and only strayed from the confines of the estate when they really had to.

I was in Germany for the first time ever, and I suppose as with all postings I treated this one as a big adventure. Obviously, some were better than others. But I was determined to learn a little of the lingo and get involved with the German way of life as much as was possible. This did not take too long, and while the other chefs were playing their game of trumps I was sat in the ladies' rest room listening to the conversation and trying to understand what the others were talking about. I was very fortunate to have a middle-aged lady working in the kitchen who, because of being married to an English soldier, could speak fluent English, and another who was learning, so there was no doubt that we could help each other when it became beyond us.

The time spent in Germany meant that we were

involved in a number of exercises. It was something of a shock to the system that, because of being an armoured regiment, we were all self-contained, and therefore the chefs were employed in humping fuel from the vehicle carrying the supplies to the armoured vehicles, mainly Chieftains, and I can assure you that by the end of that exercise I had muscles that would have done Geoff Capes proud, or so I thought!

Suddenly all the previous whinges about getting up early in order to cook breakfast seemed to fade into obscurity as we realised that the smell of tea brewing or eggs frying in evil-smelling cheap cooking oil was perhaps marginally better than the work involved in replenishing these iron-clad fighting machines.

On our return from the exercise there were all the usual debriefings and commotion that went with getting the regiment back into the clean and tidy state that the German public had become accustomed to seeing. Usually one of the most daunting tasks was that of cleaning the cooking equipment. After two weeks of solid use there was a definite build-up of jellified grease that would require removal before the next exercise went under way. Of course this time there was none of that, because we had not been using the usual burners that snorted out fire like the dragon that has been woken from his winter sleep, and if not carefully watched would easily burn the bottom of every pot placed in its path.

The fuel used to cook on in the field was an

extremely volatile mixture of petrol and air both under pressure and it was always the thing that even the bravest of soldiers, except of course the chefs, would steer well clear of. During our training we were taught all the N.S.P.s (Normal Safety Precautions) and they were drummed into your head. It is really similar to driving a car – as soon as you have passed your test the arms start to cross on the steering wheel and all the dangerous habits come into play. These burners were no exception to the rule, and the sight of a young Private or Lance Corporal letting the petrol spurt out under pressure and haphazardly throwing a lighted match in the vicinity without first checking wind direction was the cause of many a cook losing eyebrows and facial hair. Still, it would save shaving for a few days.

As time went on, more efficient equipment came in and each unit had its own modernised trucks that had been revamped into what they thought was the ultimate mobile kitchen, until, that is, they were posted to their next unit, where that truck had an even better feature of some kind or other.

Of course there was always the regiment who, for reasons that I could not figure out, never seemed to go on exercise, and it wasn't until much later on in my career that I realised how lucky I was with the number of exercises that I myself had attended – indeed, very few, but I was not complaining.

There are probably two words that any soldier who served in Germany had nightmares over, that's if he could get any sleep worrying about whether it was going to be that night or the next. The words in question are CRASH OUT. I can almost feel the ground around you shaking with the very thought of it – that is, of course, if you know what it is that I am talking about!

Before the end of the Cold War it was a necessity to be ready for an invasion from the Eastern Bloc countries into the West, and a 'crash-out' explained quite well the activity of being roused from your bed at some unearthly hour by a loud siren that blasted out around the whole garrison and the majority of the civilian town. There would, you would think, be an excuse if you slept through the sound of the klaxon but that eventuality had been adequately covered by a very complex system that worked by one of the guard waking a delegated member of the block of flats that you were living in and getting a signature to ensure that he was awake. He in turn was responsible for doing the same to the rest of the block. This always proved to be a satisfactory system.

Once we had turned out and arrived at the camp in the specified time the population of the camp seemed to be working like an ants' nest that had been stirred up with a stick, with everyone involved trying to rebuild it. But they were merely loading trucks and supplies for the move out of camp ready to set up in battle positions for the oncoming invasion.

The fact that we only left the camp once had come to make it slightly predictable, but anyway everyone tended to know when it was about to happen because the German population had to be informed of the tank movements, and therefore the dates of mobilisation were published in the local paper. If you had a good bunch of workers in the kitchen, they would let you know long before that siren released its low dulcet tones.

All the equipment that was required for the eventuality of a crash-out had to be kept in the confines of the kitchen and therefore was always a subject for an on the spot inspection, and what makes it laughable was that because we never moved out of camp the kit never became unpacked so it was the same as the last time it was inspected.

Once all the activity on a crash-out had reached its height, the stand-down siren went off. Now it was the cooks turn; the Master Chef would walk in the kitchen and say, 'The C.O. wants breakfast in an hour.'

Of course there was always the possibility that you did not know the crash-out was imminent, and the usual number to be fed at breakfast was around the 100 mark, whereas now here you were with the whole regiment to feed. The bacon was in a nice solid lump in the freezer, there were only 360 eggs, and there were various other problems for you to overcome. Invariably you did, but it was only through these sort of events that I gained the sort of experience that was needed to feed the hungry troops during the Gulf War later in my career.

For those of you who are pondering on the 'shortage of eggs' problem, I will try to enlighten you on the simplicity of making 30 eggs feed 100 men. Firstly crack the eggs and beat into a scrambled egg mix, then cut the crusts from four loaves of bread and beat the rest into the egg mix. This is then cooked in the usual way, and the bread is tasteless and expands the volume of the eggs fourfold.

This particular kitchen that I was now working in was at one time a stable, and because of that fact and because it was also adjacent to the existing stable, we had a rodent problem. By this I mean rats! It was always my pet hate to be on early shift on my own because this meant that you were responsible for opening up the kitchen, and at five in the morning it is very dark. On opening the kitchen door, it was required of you to walk about five steps into the building in order to switch on the lights. As soon as the lights were on there were always four or five of the creatures that the Pied Piper had obviously left behind. We were always capturing them, and as we only had the old-type rat traps that did not kill the creatures, they had to be killed by us. I always remember that we had a chart in our rest room that showed all the relevant details like who killed it, how long it took and how exactly the dirty deed was done. Of course, these days strict legislation does not allow for kitchens to have any sort of infestations, let alone rats.

I soon gained advancement and was moved into the Sergeants' Mess to work, and there met another group of German workers, and one in particular sticks in my mind even to this day. She had over the years gained the name of Mutti, which roughly translated means Mum, and although her apparent old age had slightly restricted her vocal cords she could still be understood purely by her expressions, and woe betide you if she was upset. To say the kitchen was put into turmoil was an understatement. But then this is what made life in the Army so varied and exciting. There was always something that made going to work in the mornings that little bit different and although when I look back we all used to moan about this that and the other, it really was enjoyable.

It was while I was in the Sergeants' Mess that I had a phone call from the Master Chef, a Warrant Officer Class Two, and was informed that on a particular date in the near future the officer in charge of the Records Office would be visiting, and asked if I would like an interview. I replied the same as the majority of chefs had answered, with a firm 'Yes'. These were always a favourite for the average chef to voice his opinions as to how he thought his career was 'progressing' and how he was aware that this was not really the case. This indeed was how I saw it, and on the day in question I waited outside the office that had been allocated to this Major for his use.

I made some last-minute adjustments to my dress as the door opened and the officer asked me in. I marched smartly the three steps to the front of the desk and was told to relax and take a seat.

The question that was next to leave the lips of the Major shook me in my boots: 'Where is your stripe?' After what seemed like an age, I answered that I had not yet been promoted, at which he seemed a little bemused, and looked again at the file in front of him. 'According to this document you have been a

Lance Corporal for two months.' There had apparently been a mix up at some point that prevented the promotion list from reaching the regiment.

The Major then asked me what I wished to see him about and I of course, after the previous news, had to tell him that my queries had already been answered.

Blues & Royals Sergeants' Mess Ball 1975

CHAPTER 4

There was a major celebration in the NAAFI that night because I was not the only one who had received this good bit of news. There was another Private, a friend of mine, who had also been overlooked at a result of this administrative error.

I did of course have to wait a few days before I could actually put the khaki embroidered chevron onto the right sleeve of all my uniforms, because the Commanding Officer has, of course, got to find time to fit you in to his busy schedule, and not when you want to be there.

The day finally came when I marched into the large ornately decorated office that an officer of his stature is entitled to, and I halted smartly in front of the desk. I was dressed in my best uniform with the grey-rimmed hat with the polished peak, and the buttons that were attached to the side of the hat glinted in the morning sunlight that shone in from the window behind the daunting figure who occupied the desk.

I marched out around five minutes later as Lance Corporal, and believe me I was as proud as punch. There is very little in the world that feels quite as good as promotion, especially in the Armed Forces.

On returning to the kitchen the looks that I received were varied and the comments as bad, the usual things like 'Where was the raffle?' and 'Who drew the lucky dip?', and the odd remark of 'They will make anyone up these days.' These were all taken in my stride because it really did not matter. The hardest part of being an NCO is learning to give orders instead of taking them.

As time went on there was a lot that I learnt and it was not only in the field of catering that this was relevant, because unknown to me until now the Army held a lot more in store for me than just a job.

The moment that you set eyes on the media advertisements to join the Army you realise that there are a lot of really good points involved in becoming a member of one of the most efficient armies of the present day. We have all heard the catch phrase 'Join the Army and see the world,' and believe me when you take up the offer there is every possibility that you will visit a number of varied and interesting places as I have. Of course the old jokes about seeing the world whilst sweeping a drill square in Aldershot will always be in the mind of the cynics, but the good times seem to outweigh the bad especially when you are soaking up the sun on a sub-tropical island half way up the Eastern Australian Coast.

I myself managed to visit a total of 12 different countries during my career and this does not include stopovers on long flights.

The three years at Detmold were disappearing behind me at a great rate of knots, and the fears that I had of living in a different country had proved to be unfounded, because once you had found your way around there was nothing that could not be mastered including the language.

The thing that I remember most about the German towns was Christmas time, when, even though the decorations did not differ much from home, the atmosphere was more electric and made you more aware that Christmas was really with you. In the traditional market square were stalls with large ginger biscuits decorated with the German words for Merry Christmas, and other delicacies, hanging round, lit up with glistening fairy lights, and there was the sound of wind organs playing the Christmas songs that are known worldwide, such as 'Stille Nacht'.

Another fond memory that I shall always carry with me is that when you were shopping in the towns and coffee was on the agenda the calorie-heavy gateaux and tartlets and other goodies that were supplied for the good of the waistline (or not so good as some would have it) were beyond comparison.

One thing is for sure – Germany has a lot to offer, especially on the sightseeing front. I paid visits to places that, if I had not been posted there, I would probably never have seen, such as two of the great dams that were destroyed by the Dambuster Squadron in the Second World War. Probably the most poignant visit was one I made in the north of the country to the now deserted Belsen concentration camp, where so many innocent Jews lost their lives in the Holocaust. The thoughts that go through your mind are unexplainable, and the whole site gives you an incredible feeling of death. There is a theory that no bird will ever fly over the location, and when you visit the site that is the way it looks. The large brick-built chambers that took the lives of those thousands of men, women and children will forever be etched on my mind.

The three years that I stayed at Detmold seemed to be passing before my eyes and there were all sorts of exercises and schemes that were taking place. One that caught the interest of the majority of the unit was to Canada. The rigmarole of all the jabs for this, that and the other left us feeling like a pin cushion, but when I look back, the month long trip to Canada, the land of the beaver and the Rockies, was well worth it. I feel that at this stage it is well worth saying that the initial feelings that invaded my mind at the beginning of my service career had long since disappeared and had been taken over by the certainty that this was a good life, and one to which I was very quickly, and easily, adapting.

Another daunting prospect was now appearing on the horizon, my first trip to Northern Ireland – a four-month tour of duty in West Belfast away from the family, and with only the quick-thinking wits and a length of gun metal between you and possible death.

This may well sound pessimistic, but it is certainly the way that I was thinking. Of course, we all hoped for a lot of luck to accompany us on the trip.

Unfortunately, our unit was not blessed with the good fortune to return to our loved ones with the same number that had departed. One of our unit was shot by sniper fire and another was shot by one of our own men who, whilst on duty in the sentry tower, had cracked under the pressure of the four-hour shift and opened fire on the camp below.

This unfortunate incident lost us two lives as the soldier then turned the rifle on himself and did the ultimate. The feelings that go through a unit when it loses one or more of its members is the same of that a family suffers when losing a loved one, and everyone is drawn together.

There were, of course, other feelings that went with the tour including the humorous. During the tour it was a necessity to ensure that, when you left a building, you were adorned with a heavy flak jacket to give you a limited protection against the sniper that might well be watching the activities from the hills that surrounded the camp. It was also the rule that you always carried your personal weapon, and what was known as 'skeleton order', which comprised webbing straps attached to which were two ammunition pouches holding the issued magazines, complete with rounds, and also a first aid dressing strapped to the belt for easy release in case of injury.

This kit accompanied me at every move within the camp and lay beside my bed for easy reach if needed. While on this tour I was on night shift, which was a 12-hour shift starting at nine and finishing the following morning. This was the shift that fed the guard, and, it seemed, anyone else who happened to drop in, with bacon sarnies and other such delicacies.

It was during one of these shifts that I made a blunder that, had Jeremy Beadle been around, would have made me a star. I was busy at the time making some 200 pasties and the only company that I had was a small radio, although what was on it was only in my subconscious. I suddenly became aware of the siren sounding; this was the warning that a mortar attack was either imminent or already taking place, and the drill was to grab the equipment that I mentioned previously and head for a large thick block-built wall, named very aptly the 'blast wall'. There were a number of these positioned around the camp and at this moment I was heading for the nearest. I swung open the door to the kitchen and ran out into the night only to find complete silence. I was, to say the least, slightly baffled until, that is, I returned to the kitchen to find the record that was blasting out on the music box was 'The Ballad of Bonnie and Clyde'! To say I felt a little foolish was an understatement, and it took a fair while before I owned up to this slight error of judgement.

The short period of 'rest and recuperation' in the middle of the tour was a welcome break for all of us, and revitalised the system with the amber nectar that the rule books had restricted to two cans a day during our stay in Ireland. The hardest part, of course, was returning to the country for the next six weeks not knowing who or what was around the next corner.

One of the duties that I had to endure whilst in Northern Ireland was an attachment to the Crumlin Road Jail. This is a civilian establishment, and the home of some of the world's most hardened terrorists and criminals. It is the Army's policy to provide a small military guard to man the watch towers, known in military jargon as Sangers, and it was my job to feed this small pocket-sized group. During this time, I made the acquaintance of a few of the civilian prison warders. I found it a very interesting few days and on a visit to the prison kitchens (I had my own small kitchen) it was a peculiar feeling to be actually in among the prisoners that made up the population of this stone-built fortress.

I was only in the Crumlin Road a week before my Armoured Personnel Carrier arrived to pick me up and return me to the friendly faces of my own unit.

The huge green armour-plated war machine has slits for the driver to see through, only around two-inches wide. It often sent my mind wondering how they drive these monstrous beasts because they could not possibly have the good all-round vision that other vehicles have. This particular vehicle had earned the nickname of a pig because of the visual appearance. It was indeed the shape of a pig's face, and I found that to travel in the back with no vision made you as sick as a pig!

On return to my unit I immediately applied for a return visit, but to my annoyance I was given a stint in the Officers' Mess, with a friend of mine, another Lance Corporal. Both of us were under the direction of the Cook Sergeant who, in those days, had the reputation of being an evil bastard if crossed, and if by some unfortunate coincidence you were in the kitchen when he staggered out of the mess after downing the whole of his four-months' supply of two beers a day in that afternoon then you had better hope that all was in order. This man was an obnoxious hypocritical swine and soon put my colleague on the C.O.'s mat when, after obtaining a few beers himself, he decided to try and cut off one of the Sergeant's hands on the servery that night instead of the medium-rare piece of topside beef that was sat on the chopping board. But then that's what man management was all about in that era. Thankfully it has now changed, and the days of hauling a young Private round the back and making him accidentally walk into your fist have long gone. Of course, there is still evidence that this form of treatment is favoured among the old school and indeed it can work and did work for a lot of military managers.

It was while I was in Northern Ireland that I became a father for the second time, and I was in the fortunate position of being sent back to

Germany for a further piece of rest and recuperation to look after my elder daughter who at that time was only two. I was the envy of all my peers not because I had become a father but because I had an extra bit of leave.

The four months were almost up when the chefs in the satellite kitchens that were spread all over Belfast started to receive better rations than we had at any previous time in the four months. It was not until much later in my career that I realised this was a case of improper food accounting. It suddenly dawned on me during a lesson that arose on my catering management course that the fault the instructor was talking about was exactly what had happened in Northern Ireland, a sure case of feast and famine. In simple terms the accountant, in this case the Master Chef, was trying not to overspend, but was being a little too frugal, and at the end of the period had too much money and had to spend it. This would easily explain why the Junior Ranks' Mess were eating fresh salmon steaks instead of mince and dumplings for the last two weeks.

After a feverish cleaning process the camp looked, I am sure, 100% better than when we arrived and I am convinced that when the next crew manned the kitchen they would leave it even cleaner than we had. After four months with this hutted assembly being home, it was time to bid farewell to the civilian artisans who had helped us by being friendly and putting their lives at risk simply by turning up for work. They had also been prepared to do some shopping for the things that were just that little bit out of our reach, such as birthday presents, because apart from a small canteen run by a couple of Indian gentlemen and known to everyone as the Chogies, there was nowhere for us to buy such things.

There was by no means any prejudice between us and the gentlemen who provided us with a service even if the profit margin was higher than the average.

The trip to Aldergrove airport in Belfast was one of jubilation, because in a short time we would be airborne and on our way back to Germany, and although the unit had suffered losses which we could not forget, we were all a lot happier to be out of that particular country.

One of the benefits of being in a place like Northern Ireland is that you always get a good stint of leave, and in this case it was three weeks for the whole unit, less of course the contingent that had remained in Detmold. They had to carry on with the chores that they had become accustomed to, and take their leave after our return.

It was on one of these leave periods that I made the mistake of travelling with my family back to England on the regimental minibus. I should mention that the Household Cavalry are very strict in their dress codes, and when travelling to and from work we were always expected to wear a collar and tie. The minibus duly arrived at Hyde Park Barracks, which was the drop-off point for the passengers to embark on the rest of their journey. I disembarked from the bus nearly last, and I noticed a slight turmoil around the guardroom. As I approached, it turned out that the Provost Sergeant was not letting anyone out of camp who was not adorned with a tie! Well, after a cramped and long journey of this nature this is something you do not need, but I opened my suitcase to unravel the pile of clothes in order to find my passport to the outside world, a tie.

After this period of leave we settled back into the day-to-day running of an armoured unit as opposed to an infantry unit, which was the role that we had adopted during the tour in Ireland.

It once again became time for me to move on; I had been thinking that I still had a good six months left in Detmold when I was called into the boss's office, which was strategically placed right inside the main door of the kitchen so as to survey everyone who entered or left the kitchen.

He handed me a piece of paper which presented me with the chance to join my brother's unit, something that I had asked for months before but, as with all things in the military, you never expect to get things that you ask for. However, this time I had managed to.

I was to pack up and move to the Marchwood Military Port, and in one month! Suddenly my head was spinning with all the various things that would require consideration before I could move, such as arranging who was going to take my furniture.

Back again in England, I drove back to Southampton and pulled up in front of my new address, and found that I was now the occupant of a maisonette – this was a two-storey house on top of another two-storey house. It overlooked the military railway line that used to pick up the soldiers who worked on the military port from their married quarters and take them to work, and at the end of the day bring them home again

After the Blues and Royals, the atmosphere of a Royal Corps of Transport camp seemed slightly more relaxed but nonetheless equally efficient, and I soon fitted into the scene reasonably well and went about creating the sort of image that I hoped would gain me promotion in the not-too-distant future.

I soon found that having another member of the family in this camp made life easier because I frequented the same drinking resorts as he did and therefore made friends that little bit quicker.

I was soon employed in the Sergeants' Mess and, as always thus far, struck up a good friendship with the ladies employed as cleaners within the mess. The practical jokes that were played by me on them are too many to list, but there were quite a few, and on Regimental Dinner nights there was always the trick by one or more of the chefs of dipping one hand in the flour bin unknown to the waitresses bedecked in their smart black skirts. Next followed a playful smack by the chef on the rump of the waitress as she departed, laden with full plates of desserts and aptly decorated with a clear white handprint on the relevant place. This happened at nearly every dinner night that I worked on and of course there was always the problem that one of the ladies would not see the funny side but we were always careful and studied the victim to see that she could 'take a joke'.

It always amazed me that no one in the dining room ever made a song and dance about it, but after going up through the ranks and reaching the status that permitted me to dine in what every Senior Non-Commissioned Officer would describe as a very exclusive club, I soon discovered that, although there was a lot of formality, much the same sort of trickery was taking place around the highly polished oak table that was the centre piece of the mess dining room. I will go into this in more detail later in these memoirs.

One of the things that every soldier, man or woman, has to endure twice a year is something that has been known to throw even the hardest warrior into an immediate cold sweat, and it is simply three letters – BFT, otherwise known as Basic Fitness Test. Those of you who have no trouble in running the annual London Marathon may well find our fears puzzling. The test involves running a measured mile and a half in fifteen minutes as a squad, and the second mile and a half in eleven and a half minutes. Easy, I hear you say, and so it was when I was 18, but I was now in my early 20s and the measured course was around the port, the run usually took part at the break of dawn, and whether or not the PT instructors had a friend in God I never knew, but it would always be a day when the wind was blowing in off the sea straight into our faces. This slowed us down by just enough for me to pass the line in eleven minutes thirty-seven seconds, causing me fair discomfort and of course a rerun tomorrow.

Oh well, never mind, it will be easier then; the wind will have changed.

The next day the wind was coming from exactly the same place and causing the same problems except this time I cut off ten seconds and passed. I suppose it was the thought of extra PT at seven every morning that gave me the enthusiasm to become a world-class sprinter. When the instructor was shouting 'eleven twenty' down the course, I was around 50 yards from the end post. This test took place twice yearly and as soon as the first six-monthly period had expired there were always the keen fitness freaks who were lined up at the start ready to be the first to be passed fit for the second six months of the year.

There is also in the Army another set of three letters that put the proverbial chill into the backbone of the less energetic breeds such as the Army Catering Corps and for that matter any of the non-infanteers, and this was the CFT, the Combat Fitness Test. Don't ask me how, but in the twenty-one years that I served my Queen and Country I always managed to be busy and avoid this menacing run. The test itself took various forms but basically was a forced march with around 20 pounds of equipment and a weapon which weighed around 10 pounds. The course was usually around ten miles, and many a squaddie had suffered blisters and exhaustion after one of these tortuous expeditions so, considering those facts, I suppose I was quite fortunate to sidestep this gruelling test and nevertheless somehow or other get the mark that was required to say I had completed it.

Since arriving at Marchwood I had been frequenting the NAAFI more than was usual as my brother, Graham, would often leave the small room that he, as a single soldier, called his home and visit the three-bedroomed maisonette that was my habitat. His purpose was to drag me out for the customary pint of brown frothy liquid, regularly pulled from the pipes that trailed under the wooden bar and down into the cellar, which tasted better every time I lifted the glass to my lips.

It was during one of these sessions that I was to witness the nerve that my brother had stored up in his torso ready for such occasions. It was his birthday, so there were definitely more people in the bar that night. There must have been a good 12 or so people around the table in the corner, and the noise that was erupting from that region was more than the poor old jukebox could cope with, and spirits were running high. Someone then started a whip-round, and collected a sum that came to around £9.00, and then proceeded to the bar in order to fill a pint pot with a sample from every optic on the bar plus anything else that happened to come within the price. The glass was then ceremoniously placed on the old polished table in front of my one and only brother. Of course, care had to be taken not to spill this mixture as the table did not warrant having all the high-gloss varnish removed at this time.

There was the usual banter of 'Get it down, get it

down,' all done in such a musical way that the crowd at Cardiff Arms Park on finals day would have been proud of it. But! what was this? Refusal to drink? Unheard of! But he was adamant that this was not going to pass his lips. Then a female voice somehow or other was heard over the tones of the chorus, which was getting louder by the minute, and said that he was not man enough to drink it.

As if by a miracle the room went silent and the posterior of my brother was starting to raise from the chair, and on the way up the pint glass was lifted from the table. Now at this juncture I had quite naturally assumed that the last remark had indeed hurt his pride. Not a bit of it; he simply turned to the female involved and said in a quite calm tone, 'If you want it, have it!' and proceeded to pour it over her immaculately lacquered hair style. Of course, he lost a lot of credit that night not least because he had wasted £9.00 worth of treasured alcohol.

The young lady retired to her room in order to get the remains of the special cocktail out of her hair and unfortunately never returned. The evening continued with the usual party pieces being performed, and one that holds the most prominent place in my memories is that of one of the Corporals who, after finishing the beer in the straight pint pot, decided to eat the glass. Now, if this is making your hair stand up at the thought of a man actually chewing glass then you will have no problem in believing me when I say that watching this turns even the strongest stomach muscles.

I, of course, never knew how he did not end up

with serious internal injuries because he swallowed the chewed up remains of the glass!

I spent most of two years at Marchwood. As I have earlier mentioned, I was and still am a lover of the practical joke but there was one occasion that it backfired. Each morning at tea break there was the usual banter of what had happened and was going to happen and, for reasons that I cannot remember, we got around to the subject of baths and I just happened to say for a laugh that this particular lady who had broached the subject should come and wash my back. Well, this went on for weeks and I kept teasing her that she had not got the bottle and she with the same vigour said that I was all mouth, which made me say that I took my bath at six o'clock when I got home. There the subject ended, as did the tea break.

That evening as I lay relaxing in the warm water that had minutes earlier cascaded from the taps there was a knock at the front door. I did as I usually did and carried on as if I hadn't heard it, until, that is, the female who I thought would never go through with it DID, and in she walked armed to the teeth with sponge and bubble bath! To say I was embarrassed was an understatement of huge proportions and I still had to live this down the next day at work.

If there was ever a place for an autopsy the rest room of a kitchen was definitely it; whether it was the civilian workers or the military it made no difference, and I always found that if you were not in on the event that the discussion centred on then you might just as well carry on working, because there would be very little else discussed over the fragrant aroma of the tea that had stained more than its fair share of tea cups.

I remember very well the tea break that had followed a trip into the more seedy areas of Hamburg, one which, unfortunately, I did not join, but the talk next day ranged from the slightly humorous to the extremely worrying at least for the married men amongst them because no matter how hard one tries to conceal the escapades of a trip of this nature it is almost a foregone conclusion that sooner or later 'She Who Must Be Obeyed' will be the recipient of the news that divorces are made of. One of the more difficult tasks for any married man is trying desperately to wriggle out of the, and please forgive the language, 'shit', because if you are not well practised in the art then it is not too difficult to find yourself slowly but surely sinking. There is a phrase that I have not forgotten that bears witness to this, and that is, 'One is always in the shit but the depth varies,' and after a night out in a place like Hamburg this expression meant more than it usually would.

If the rest room was dominated by the single soldier, of course the discussion was of a different nature and became the place to talk over the conquests of the previous evening and how they had pulled the girls, and especially which ones.

Of course, there were always the married men who, for reasons known only to them, wandered off the straight and narrow as far as faithfulness to their spouses was concerned. One particular incident that I remember well was when, after an exercise that took the unit to another part of Germany from where we would normally be based, a Corporal who worked alongside me strayed off the path of the well behaved and met a delightful young lady (or so he thought). As time transpired there was a distinctive irritation in the more private regions of his body, so obviously he thought the worst and assumed that he had contracted some sort of affliction that reached the parts other itches couldn't.

He felt that the best thing that he could do in the circumstances was to tell his wife and confess all. If he had checked with the doctor first, the fact that a sweat rash was to blame would have saved him from the obvious torment that his better half would lay on him, knowing the truth.

The Corporals' Mess was always a good place to refresh the parts that needed refreshing, especially at lunchtime, if you did not have to return to work after an early shift. It was after one of these sessions, and of course before the drink driving laws were better enforced, that a Corporal who had seen his fair share of service and had obviously had a pint for the majority of years served, staggered blissfully down the winding staircase that led from the Corporals' Mess out into the camp itself. At this stage he donned a crash helmet and tried to throw a leg over his daily form of transport, his moped. I suppose that looking back one of us who were looking on with humorous thoughts should have stopped him, but we didn't.

He started the engine and revved it a lot higher than did it any good at all. He then dropped the clutch and, head down, pointed the bike towards the main entrance to the camp. It was at this stage that the small crowd of onlookers took a sharp intake of breath as the rider headed at a fair lick toward the metal bar that was positioned at waist height across the road! What followed next would have, if I had had a video camera, won me a large sum of money. The Corporal hit the barrier and was left swinging unhurt over the bar like a towel over a radiator waiting to dry; the bike proceeded across the road and ended its short journey in the hedge. There were a good many such events, or ones that were similar, but far too trivial to mention in these memoirs.

CHAPTER 5

After a two-year stint at Marchwood I was promoted to Corporal and posted to Farnborough, in the sticks of Hampshire, and a large training regiment of the Royal Engineers. This had without a doubt the largest kitchen that I had ever had the pleasure to serve in. At the peak time during the two years that I was there we were feeding 1,500 men three meals a day, a job that was blessed with the problems of any big kitchen, especially when the equipment was always breaking down, and considering that this was a fairly new kitchen this was far too regular an occurrence. I was starting this posting in a new place with a new rank and I suppose that as everyone does I went into the job with guns blazing thinking that I was the only one who has ever reached the rank of Corporal, but fear not, I was soon put in my place, and within a few days came to realise that I was only as good as the team around me. If that sounds pompous then I apologise, but it is a fact that if the ones you are working with are duds then the job will only ever be second class.

I had only been at this unit a couple of days when, at around four in the morning, there was a loud hammering on the door of my eight-foot-by-eight-foot room, and as I thought I was dreaming, I ignored it and turned over in the position that lent itself best to me finishing the night in the same peaceful slumber that it had started. But the banging returned a few seconds later, so like something from the film of the same name I rose like a zombie and reached out for the door handle, which took a few seconds to open because I had locked it before retiring.

Standing outside the door was one of the Guard, looking as if it might well have been a bad idea to have woken me, and in a very feeble voice he muttered something that did not, perhaps, sink into the grey matter as fast as it should have. After a repeat version of the phrase I realised that I had been summoned to the guardroom. This usually meant Bad News, especially at this time of the night, and as always the thoughts of members of the family being injured or even worse ploughed through my mind without any of the problems that I had met in comprehending the original message. As quickly as I could I threw on a pair of jeans and tee shirt and made my way to the brightly lit guardroom and opened the door, to be confronted by a Military Policeman standing behind the polished wood counter that separated 'us' from 'them', so to speak. After I had given my name and rank, not necessarily in that order, I was immediately told to get myself into that cell.

This I can assure you was not the reception that I had imagined and as the large steel door adorned in the centre with a spy hole opened I entered with unease. What was before me was totally unexpected; sat on the bench and hard wooden bed were the rest of the unit's unmarried chefs who lived in the barracks and the only thing, apart from that, which we had in common was that none of us knew why we were there .

It was a good hour before the first of us was called from the cell by a plain-clothes Military Policeman on detachment to the Special Investigation Branch (SIB), and after he was interviewed it was my turn. I was led into another cell, still unaware as to what this was all about. I was told to sit on the polypropylene blue chair in front of a plain wooden table that had a plain buff-coloured folder on it, and was asked the usual questions: Number? Rank? Name? After this the interviewer immediately started putting words into my mouth and it soon became apparent that the reason we were all imprisoned the way we were was because overnight someone had entered the kitchen unauthorised and made themselves a midnight snack. This was a regular occurrence but this particular night there was an over-enthusiastic officer on duty who decided to call in external investigators and add a little bit of intrigue to the situation.

Believe me, I tried to tell the gent on the other side of the desk that if a chef had wanted to do this he would purely have drawn the keys from the guardroom and let himself in – Easy! But this did not convince him. He knew it was me – he had my boot print embedded in a patch of grease on the floor. It was at this stage that I laughed, and looking back it was probably not the most sensible thing that I had ever done, but to explain to you, there were around 22 chefs working in that kitchen and we all wore the same non-slip boots – that is, except me! As I had just arrived from a maritime unit I had a different sole. When this was shown, I was excluded from the investigation, but the most humorous part of the whole affair was that the Monkees, as the MPs were known, had cordoned off the patch of grease still believing that a chef had done the dirty deed.

It lay there until lunchtime with the authorities still trying to prove that a proper crime had been committed when an over-enthusiastic soldier threw a bucket of boiling water over the evidence and completely destroyed it. The hours passed, and the alleged crime was never mentioned again.

This was one of the most exceptional and diverse units that I had served in during my career and I knew that this was the case when an enthusiastic officer suggested that the chefs, of whom there were around 20, should take part in an exercise and act as platoon commanders and do what proper soldiers do. Now, we had all been trained in basic fieldcraft but of course being chefs had very little interest in the phrase 'a soldier first, a chef second', especially when I was up to my thighs in freezing cold muddy water in the woods at Hawley near Farnborough. This represented a jungle, and obviously had the feel as this was the location chosen by the TV production crew for the filming of *It Ain't Half Hot, Mum.*

As darkness drew around us, I knew that this was probably a good time to put my map-reading and compass skills into practice, and on doing this I realised just how little I actually knew about this area of soldiering. Although the exercise only lasted a day and night and was enjoyed by all, it was an experience that I for one had had enough of.

This was the only unit where the Master Chef, who I suppose was after a mention in the Honours list, had arranged for the unit chefs to produce a number of meals on wheels each day. These meals, known to the whole of the kitchen staff as 'muck on a truck', left the kitchen in a specially designed green box with a metal case sat in the bottom that contained a lump of smouldering charcoal in order to keep the food warm, and I suppose that it did as we never had any complaints.

The meals were picked up by volunteer ladies who seemed to think, looking back, that they could have what they wanted, but of course, although we were providing a service to the old folk, at the time it was just an inconvenience to us.

This was a very modern camp and had a beautiful indoor swimming pool and other luxuries such as a sauna and a wonderfully equipped gymnasium, and this made the prospect of spending two years in the establishment a better one.

It was while I was serving here that the law of averages was broken because it was usual that only Lance Corporals and Privates did the task of Duty Chef, but here I was, a Corporal doing not only Duty Chef but Night Cook as well. It sort of made me think, what would I be doing as a Sergeant if ever I reached that pinnacle?

Night shift in this establishment meant that invariably you had the daunting task of turning two sacks of carrots into baton shapes, one and a quarter inches by a quarter by a quarter, or trimming the dead leaves off two sacks of Brussels sprouts, and that was on top of all the other tasks like blanching off a total of eight sacks of potatoes that earlier in the day had been lovingly cut into the familiar shape of a chip. This was the staple diet of the average British squaddie, and believe me if there were no chips on the menu then mutiny could very easily have erupted. I say 'was' because in recent years there has been an upsurge of the healthy eating and there has definitely been a swerve towards the pasta and baked jacket potatoes as the media do their bit in telling us that no matter what we eat sooner or later it will be bad for us.

Perhaps this is a good a time as any to let you take a short look at just what the typical soldier would eat in a normal day, both in his base camp and while on exercise or scheme. Breakfast in the majority of British Army camps can consist of a selection of cereals ranging from the rather plain cornflakes to the more exotic muesli type; this could be followed by bacon, sausage, eggs, baked beans, tomato and fried bread or toast, all washed down with tea or coffee. This is, of course, the whole menu, but the soldier can have as much as he would like. This is a far cry from the days when you could only have one rasher of bacon or one sausage and you were restricted to a quarter of a pint of milk on your cereal.

Lunch would normally offer around five choices, items such as Cornish pasties, spaghetti Bolognese, a fish dish and two others, and on top of that there was a salad bar.

The hot dishes were, as I have said, served with a choice of boiled, chipped or baked jacket potatoes and a choice of vegetable, usually peas or baked beans. There was always fresh fruit and yoghurts, and in the latter years there was also the introduction of a cheeseboard.

The evening meal was usually a roast meal with steaks almost every night and perhaps a curry. This was accompanied by two or three choices of potatoes and numerous varieties of vegetables, and finished off with usually five or six choices of hot and cold sweets. As time went on, of course, trends changed and I suspect that if you happened to do a stint of National Service in the '50s, then this would not have been the style that would have been displayed on the hotplate in those days!

Of course there were always the special occasions that happened in every camp throughout the British

Army, whether abroad or at home in the British Isles, and these could be in the shape of an ordinary Sergeants' Mess function right up to a visit by Royalty – although I catered for a number of the aristocracy during my service, the only member of the Royal Family that I ever met through actually cooking was the Duchess of York. This was later, during my tour of duty in Berlin, at a time when she was still married to His Royal Highness Prince Andrew, and I was very honoured to be put in charge of the preparation and cooking for the small select gathering.

There were also the elaborate Officers' Mess Balls, and these are always an eye-opener, especially for the visitor who has never seen a full Army Catering Corps buffet. To say that it is prepared in a few hours would be the understatement of the year. It usually took a team of three or four people three days to prepare the food, and that of course does not take into consideration the planning and ordering, and ensuring in the middle of winter that the Commanding Officer can have his fresh strawberries from Kenya – at a price, of course.

It was a great learning time for the newer chef, and it was always a time when the team involved tried to do better than the last buffet that was prepared for that particular function.

There was a vast list of different occasions throughout the year, from the Burns Supper in January to the Bonfire Night Bar-b-que in November, and in the average unit there were at least three or four Christmas functions, so the chefs were a very busy team, and because of the unsociable hours they worked, the tedious tasks of guard duties were left to the rest of the unit. There were of course the exceptions. Some units had the Senior Non-Commissioned Officers of the kitchen doing Orderly Sergeant and Orderly Officer, but fortunately they were few and far between.

The food served on exercise was usually very good and nutritious, but I am sure that some people who read this and were not blessed with belonging to the beloved Corps will not agree. There was always the compo – this was a type of foodstuff that you either liked a lot or you hated, and it did have one very efficient quality. It was an extremely good binding agent. Compo was usually tinned or dehydrated food that could be eaten cold and straight from the tin if required. In a scenario where the unit was on the move at all times this was a very necessary part of the catering repertoire. In times of hostilities such as the Gulf War, when we were stopping only at night, there was no way that a cooker could be lit up and used, as the light would be able to be seen by the enemy many miles away.

Of course there was the odd exercise where fresh food was combined with the compo, and believe me the chefs performed minor miracles with the rations that they were given, but although for the majority of the time the troops were happy, it was impossible to please everyone.

New ideas were always being tested, and if an ingredient was missing, then it showed just what sort of calibre the chef was if he could make a dish with a substitute ingredient. It was quite often the case that a dish such as lasagna had the vital pasta missing, and we would make pancakes to replace the layers that made up a good dish of the Italian favourite. Most of the time the troops eating it could not tell the difference.

I did not really enjoy my stay at Farnborough, but it did have its advantages in that I met my wife Ann there, and she willingly accompanied me to my next posting in Lisburn, in Northern Ireland.

It was usual for the husband to precede the wife on these or any other postings until a married quarter could be made available. This was so in my case and I had a month of living as a single man until my wife could fly out and join me.

The first time that we walked into our house led to a certain amount of fear, as we were now part of the Irish community, and to say the one and a half miles that I had to cycle to work was nerve-racking was a definite understatement. The thought that a simple bike ride could result in a sniper's bullet winging its way towards me is not my idea of starting the day off right.

Of course, once I had been checked at the gate and had the obligatory searches made I was allowed entry into the camp, so all I then had to concern myself with was the safety of my wife, who was not accustomed to the terrorist threats and other aspects that made life in Northern Ireland so different from the life of the average British squaddie anywhere else in the world.

The life of an Army wife is very demanding and is

not easy to handle, especially if you have not before had to settle in new surroundings and make friends with people that you have never met. My wife, Ann, always handled the situation to the best of her ability, and although I think that I knew she was not the happiest that she had been in her life, she coped very well with the hardships that were always abundant for any soldier's wife.

Once at work, the kitchen ran the same as all the other kitchens that I had been in, apart from the fact that there were patrols coming in off the streets at all hours who required feeding or at the very least a cup of hot tea. To be perfectly honest, despite the extra work I would not have changed places with the squaddie on the streets of Belfast or any other city in the province.

We quickly settled into our new and to some extent dangerous lifestyle, and soon made new friends, but as it turned out the tour was very short-lived, and I was soon called upon to rap on the Catering Officer's door to receive some good news – or at least it should have been. The Captain was seated behind the large polished wooden desk, and looked up and smiled as I entered the office. The thought of a bollocking flew from my mind – that smile meant good news, or so I thought.

I listened to the words that sprang from the officer's lips, and I could feel the excitement building up inside as he told me that I had been promoted to the rank of Sergeant; but then, as with all snippets of good news, came the catch.

To take advantage of this promotion meant a

four-month trip to the other side of the world, to the islands that had been fought for two years earlier and retaken from the Argentinians. 'The Falklands,' I can hear you thinking, 'what's bad about that?'. Well, under normal circumstances nothing, I suppose, but this would mean that I would miss the birth of my expected baby, and what was worse, I still had to inform my wife; this decision needed to be a joint one, because it affected her as much as me, if not more.

The journey home that evening was horrendous. I must have been through how I was going to break the news a hundred times, but on my arrival at the front door the female perception was working overtime. The first thing that passed her lips was, 'What's wrong?' and all the things that had been subconsciously planned on the cycle ride between the camp and the quarter disappeared from my mind, and I was left stuttering excuses on the doormat. It is usual in these cases that the female partner bursts into tears and this was no exception to the rule.

It was not so much the thought of me going to the Falklands that bothered her but the fact that I would miss the birth of our baby, and when I look back I realise that my wife handled the situation entirely selflessly, because she said if it meant that I would get my promotion then I had better go.

It is this sort of reaction that makes an Army wife a good one, along with the fact that while the husband is at work when a move is imminent, the wife is at home filling the plywood boxes with rope handles at the end which are supplied for the use of Army families moving from one country to the other. The Army wife, it must be said, has to put up with a great deal of discomfort and is often without the one thing that makes for a good marriage, a partner. Her husband is usually away from the family home for at least three months of the year, and in addition guard duties remove him from his responsibilities as the householder for at least one night a month unless, like me, he is very lucky. I mean that during my 21 years in the service I can count on my two hands the number of guard duties that I did. But then again, I did more than my fair share of Duty Cooks, so I suppose although they did not last all night, they were still a millstone around the chef's neck.

It was usually the case, however, that once a chef hit the rank of Sergeant, or as it was known, Senior Rank status, the duties changed, and he would become a Guard Commander and not part of the Guard itself, but even these duties were very rare, and only put onto the chefs if the Commanding Officer thought that the chefs should assist his own Regimental Senior Non-Commissioned Officers. In my case this happened only twice, so I must quite honestly admit that I was one of the lucky ones as far as duties were concerned. Of course, my wife did not see it that way – to her any duty was one too many, and I suppose that was common in every married quarter in the country.

The rigmarole that goes with vacating a quarter on a move is enough to reduce even the strongest man to tears. Naturally the house has to be clean, to be fair to the incoming occupants, but the Army expects it to be in 'as new' condition, or there is a bill raised to bring in a team of cleaners to do what you apparently had not done to their satisfaction.

This of course was left mostly to the lady of the house unless the husband had enough leave left to assist his wife in the tedious job of housework, and if the couple had children then it made life even more difficult for the wife to cope. They deserved a medal, each and every one of them. For those who do not realise just how far the inspection went, when I left the 12 or so quarters that I occupied I had dismantled and cleaned every cooker that each house held, and I mean dismantled. Each part was degreased and cleaned and put aside ready for rebuild. Once this had been done, usually in the last couple of days, we lived on Pot Noodles and McDonalds' takeaways until the handover of the house, known to the Army as the 'march out'.

There were always the moans that the house was cleaner on 'march out' than on 'march in', and in a lot of cases that was true, but the pride of the housewife in her own house made it that way and without being biased, this was very true with my wife.

The Army wife is indeed a rare breed and I believe it is true to say that without the support that the wives gave their spouses the British Army would be a mere shadow of its present glory.

CHAPTER 6

The time between the point where I made the decision to go to the Falklands and the point where I was waiting in the departure lounge at Royal Air Force station Brize Norton was, or seemed to be, very short indeed, and there was the normal tearful farewell that always accompanied a five-month tour away from the loved ones. While they were always in our minds and could never be totally forgotten, they had to be hidden in a part of the mind that did not interfere with what made the individual soldier, even a chef, a Lean Mean Fighting Machine.

Once the parents and wives had all gone their separate ways there we all were, the team, and ready to get on and try and forget the tears that had trickled down the flushed cheeks of wives and mothers. This was what happened in most cases and it was sometimes a relief when you had said your goodbyes!

As the VC10 lifted its huge silver-grey fuselage off the tarmac that formed the runway, I felt the familiar surge of nausea running through my body, and I knew that I should have to fight against the need to use the polythene-lined bag that was housed in the net on the rear of the seat in front of me.

It was a long flight to the Ascension Islands, where we were transferred to the ex–British Rail ferry that was to transport us to the Falkland Islands, to the bay where so many of our brave colleagues had lost their lives on board the Sir Galahad. That incident was in the war for the recovery of the Islands from the Argentinians, which had been fought only two years earlier.

To say that the journey was top class would not be fair to the class system. The first seven days of the ten-day journey were, for me, spent 'speaking down the big white telephone calling for Hughie' or, for those who are not up to speed with the Army jargon, being sick as a dog. As you have probably realised by now, I am not the best traveller in the world, and for me the sooner the boat docks or the plane lands the happier I am.

Of course, there were the usual practical jokes aboard ship that took the fancy of the jokers. Within a day of leaving Ascension on our 4000-mile voyage, there on the notice board was a request for volunteers to serve on the 'Iceberg Watch' and of course, soldiers being the naive type, they started to put their names on the list. Another day there was a small piece of paper that said an extra activity had been planned for later that day, and would comprise water skiing from the back of the ship, and to my utter disbelief the names started to go up, and then the scrubbing out of the names so that mates would not recognise that they had been stupid enough to write them up in the first place.

This was the first time that I had actually worn three stripes on my uniform and I am sure that, for anyone who has served in the Forces, it is a proud moment when you put on the heavy green knitted jumper with that extra stripe on it, whether it be one two or three. All rules seem to change when you reach senior rank status; you eat in a different mess, you do different duties, and life in general seems to change for the better.

One of the hardest things I found to get used to was that, while up until this moment I had always addressed the boss by his rank, now I was being told that Dave would do; but I still called him by his rank, or 'Q', which was short for S.Q.M.S. or Squadron Quarter Master Sergeant, and it took a lot of self-training to make the change.

On arrival in the Falkland Islands we were all herded onto a large floating raft used for transporting equipment from ship to shore when it was impossible to get in close. This was apparently called a mexefloat and the hundred or so of the lads huddled together on the open deck suddenly realised that one step in the wrong direction would mean that you were taking an early bath in the sea.

As the float hit the shores of the small, almost shanty-looking town known as Port Stanley, we all surged forward in an attempt after ten days or so to be reunited with terra firma.

We were then transported to a huge block of

small rooms that had been christened with the name of Coastel. In theory this was a floating hotel with a marvellously equipped kitchen and various-sized cabins. I was sharing with another Cook Sergeant who had been there for a couple of months already; this of course meant that in a couple of months, when I was half-way through my tour, he would be leaving for home and a couple of weeks well-earned leave. There were some things that were sure to spark off the greenery of envy in any soldier, and one was someone who had finished a tour when you were only half-way through yours.

But as with all things in the Army you learned to live with your upsets as well as your celebrations. Within a few hours I found myself standing behind the stainless steel servery with the heat lamps overhead keeping the roast mutton hot and steaming, whilst the chef at the carving board was doing his best to carve great slices for the ravenous hoards that were forming the queue, spreading back to the doors at the far end of the dining room.

The kitchen aboard the Coastel was one of the best equipped that I had ever worked in, and indeed one of the cleanest, but there came with the kitchen a strange puzzle. After about three weeks of working as the kitchen manager I began to notice an odd shortage in the number of trays and metal pots that until now had adorned the kitchen shelves. A search was made of all the fridges and freezers to ensure that food being stored away was not the reason for the shortage, but to no avail.

Then one morning, whilst taking a coffee break

on the steel-meshed balcony that went around the perimeter of the vessel, I happened to notice how clear the water was, and looking down I could not believe my eyes. There sat on the bottom of the ocean was about three weeks' worth of washing up!

The story was that the ordinary soldiers who had the duties in the kitchen of washing the pots and pans had decided that if a pot could not be just swilled out and turn up clean then it should be given a good long soak in salt water.

The next job was to call in the team of divers from the Royal Engineers to retrieve that which was now showing definite signs of being fully submersed in salt water.

Even though we knew this was happening there was nothing we could do to stop it, so every month when the weather was good in would come the divers and up would come the pots and pans.

I must add that the Falklands weather was what could only be described as changeable, and it was not unusual to have snow, rain, sun and gale force winds in the same day. There were times when the wind was so strong that to walk was almost an impossibility, and everyone was leaning into the wind like aged men without their sticks. Christmas Day was brilliantly sunny and we even managed to get a bit of tanning in, but I hasten to add that this was only temporary. The next day we were back to normal.

I had been on the Island a month when I was moved to what was known as Fipass – this was shortened from Falkland Island Port and Storage

System, and in layman's terms was a floating port where huge cargo ships were loaded and unloaded with ease by the soldiers specially trained for that task. The ships arrived day after day with supplies for the civilian population as well as the military, and as these civilians had very little in the way of luxuries in the food line due to their geographic position, news travelled extremely quickly when a ship was due in with a cargo of, say, oranges or bananas and a queue quickly formed outside the local shop or store.

Yes — we have no bananas!

The trip to the Islands was almost like being in a time warp; there was a distinct feeling that I was back in the mid-1920s. There were numerous things that brought this about and the most prominent in my memory is the telephone exchange that the islanders used. It was still the little handle that was turned a number of times depending on who was trying to get through to who, and usually the operator could inform the caller whether the recipient of the call was in or out, and often even where he or she had gone. This was a sharp contrast to the high-tech operations on the outskirts of Port Stanley where, via satellite, the soldiers of the Islands phoned home to Blighty. On Christmas Day the queue was considerable, and once one was through the conversation was both exciting and saddening because, while it was wonderful to speak to loved ones, it was a real pain to be away on the day of the year that you really should be with your family whatever happens. But this was not the case, so we just had to get on and enjoy the day as much as we could.

One of the other things that made the Islands that little bit different was that everywhere was dotted with billowing puffs of peat smoke coming from the very small chimney pots that adorned the red-coloured houses around the town. Each house was allocated a plot of peat by the government and it was up to the individual to dig his own peat and keep his family warm during the cold weather.

Boxing Day was a big day for the islanders and was celebrated by a race day on the racecourse in Stanley. These were not the thoroughbred Red Rums that we see on Channel Four's racing programme, but ordinary farm horses with their owners acting as jockeys, and the only official betting was a tote operated by other islanders.

There was almost a carnival atmosphere. The sun shone, the money changed hands at a great rate, and everyone, including myself, had a good day. This was completed for me by being invited to a local house to join the family in a bar-b-que, which made a nice change from the mundane life on the Coastel.

Of course, there were a number of friendships made during the five months, but as with the majority of cases in the Services, these are soon forgotten when the next move occurs. There are the odd cases when a friendship becomes more than that, but these are very much few and far between. The saying is that you have no friends in the Army, just mates, and to some extent that is very true, because as soon as you strike up a friendly acquaintance they move or you do.

The islands were by this time building up with a strong military presence, which included an Army Ordnance Corps Bakery and a Field Hospital. There was also the large contingent of civilian contractors, who were busy building the new Mount Pleasant airfield and military accommodation. This was a huge project and I would think that no one envied the men digging trenches and the like in that weather.

Even with the new accommodation, I do not think that a posting to the Falkland Islands would be top on the popularity list of many people. The Islands are very beautiful if you are, like me, a lover of Dartmoor with its beautiful colours of the gorse and heather.

Wizard prang, old boy!

The four months on the island had its ups and downs, and certainly the news that finally arrived informing me of the birth of my daughter Lisa was a good excuse to get thoroughly wrecked in the small bar that was exclusive to the Army Catering Corps, and very aptly named the Cooks' Bar.

Wherever in the world I went in peacetime there was almost always a cooks' brand. Why not? After all, the chefs were always the first to start work and the last to finish – truly a worthy breed.

It was on this tour of duty as a newly promoted Sergeant that I attended my first Regimental Dinner. It really was a strange affair; the dress for these occasions is usually formal which meant a dinner jacket with the colour of the lapels indicating your own regiment or corps. The Catering Corps was grey and yellow, so I had grey lapels and two grey stripes down the outside of the trouser legs, all set off very smartly with a white dinner shirt and bow tie. This was recognised and known as 'mess dress', but this particular evening the dress was 'full combats', a form of dress right at the opposite end of the scale from that previously mentioned. On arrival, instead of the customary port there was a pint of bitter, and the mess was decorated with camouflage nets and Tilley lamps.

The menu consisted of a gourmet's nightmare starting with tomato soup with the main course of brown stew and dumplings and the sweet was bread and butter pudding with custard.

The only thing that did not change was the usual etiquette. Regimental Dinners were always extremely formal and each regiment that I was posted to had its own rules for how things were done, such as the passing of the port. One regiment would have it travelling around the table anticlockwise and another clockwise. Some said it was not to leave the table and others it was not to touch the table. It was considered a complete 'no-no' to leave the table, even for the purpose of relieving oneself, and the usual form of punishment if you went against the rule was 'extra duties', usually rising in handfuls of five depending on how the Regimental Sergeant Major handled the offender. There were occasions when a Senior Non-commissioned Officer would leave the table unnoticed by the hierarchy on the top table, but you could be sure that on his return the pranksters around his place would have made it extremely difficult for him to be seated because his chair would be missing.

This always started a cheer from the immediate area and thereby attracted the attention of the RSM who would hold his fist in the air and release the five fingers of the hand in short sharp bursts till he reached the number of extra duties the culprit would receive and how many he thought suitable to match the crime.

The very fact that these dinners were always so formal meant that a lot of time and preparation went into the meal that was eventually served up to the honoured guests, and it was usually the custom to produce fare that most of the diners had never tasted, and of course this meant that the chef could put his or her talent into true perspective and shine.

One saying was very true of the Army chef, and that was, 'You are only as good as your last meal,' because, believe me, if you produced a bad meal, especially at a Regimental Dinner, it would haunt you forever, but a good one, whilst it always brought praise, was forgotten before the next time.

One of the strict rules that went along with a Regimental Dinner was that after the formalities of dining you were not permitted to leave the building before the Regimental Sergeant Major, and even if you were obliged to, you had first to gain his permission, so this meant a very late, but I must say mostly enjoyable, evening, especially if you like the amber nectar.

A good many people always tried to excuse themselves from the dinner night only to be told by the RSM, 'See you tonight, Sergeant.' I found that the easiest way to get out of attendance was to be working behind the scenes – at least that way you were almost certainly assured of an early evening and NO hangover. The next morning always bore witness to those Senior NCOs who had attended – eyelids that always hung heavy, and various other signs that the overindulgence of 'falling-down water' was taking its toll.

Jim Davidson on quality control duty

It was not in the slightest way unusual to see various participants in the previous evening's events taking refuge in a quiet corner and obviously hoping that they were going to die, at least for the rest of the morning!

One of the worst experiences I came across during my service was trying to cook 300 greasy fried eggs whilst under the clutches of a huge hangover.

The Falklands taught me a lot, like never to go back if I could help it. Sure, it is a very beautiful place and the islanders are obviously very happy with their way of life, but I would suspect that, with the very large influx of soldiers now permanently based on one of the Islands, life for them can never be the same, even if they do feel more secure for having a resident protecting force.

While I was stationed in the Falklands my wife gave birth to the youngest of our three daughters, as I have mentioned, and of course as with any new father there was a feeling of relief and excitement that the wait for this new life to arrive was over, but for me there was a deep feeling of regret that I could not be there for the birth and see my new baby. For that I had to wait another month, but needless to say the Royal Mail was kept busy sending photographs across the 8,000 miles between Southampton where my wife was staying and Port Stanley where I was, and that was on top of the daily letter that I kept going for the whole five months that I was there.

The British winter brings the Falklands summer, but in these far-southern islands it is not a summer that lasts very long, and certainly not one of those seasons that gets over-warm.

I certainly enjoyed my posting to that part of the world, but of course as with all, or at least most unaccompanied postings, I was glad to get back and enjoy some well-earned rest.

My next posting was to a small village on the outskirts of Cambridge called Longstanton, and I was posted as one of the Cook Sergeants with an infantry battalion, namely the 2nd Queens, once again a very old unit and very proud of the fact, with battle honours going back as far as the Battle of Gujerat.

This was a very short posting and lasted only six months before I moved once more, and while I had a very enjoyable time with that unit, I did not do anything out of the ordinary that had not been done in previous postings. From the depths of East Anglia I moved in a south-westerly direction to Warminster, a small market town on the edge of Salisbury Plain in Wiltshire, and became attached to the School of Infantry for the next three years, and I think that looking back this was probably one of my most enjoyable postings, but not for any particular reason other than it was a fun place to be and the people that I worked with were all agreeable and good natured. It was while I was at Warminster that the Army brought in the first of a system of computers with software specially designed for the catering departments' issuing and receiving of rations, and it surprised me to find a lot of opposition to this new introduction because, although it was a great deal of work to set up the new system and many hours burning the midnight oil, the end result would be well worth it. But as with all new technology there were always the few that did not see it as this.

I, without sounding too big headed, realised that this was the way ahead, and tried to throw myself in at the deep end and learn as much as possible about the machine that was to change everything involved with the administration of the Army kitchen, from the basic stock keeping to the personal details of all the men, from the Master Chef to the storeman. The hardest part was the many hours spent burning the midnight oil trying, at first without much success, to balance the amount of stock against income and expenditure. Of course, after the first couple of months this settled down, and although there was double the amount of paper used, the critics were certainly proved wrong, and the system took over the life of the kitchen management staff. There were still the members of the old school who, if they could possibly manage it, would steer well clear of the monster with the Square Green Eye.

There were of course times in the early days when I, like a lot of novices in the areas of computer science, made the odd mistake such as 'coming out' of the system incorrectly, and leaving files open or other mishaps. I now realise why back-up tapes are so important, especially when, like me, you happen to wipe clean the entire hard disk. Whoops! And I suspect you have already guessed that I was not the most popular man on earth or even further afield for that matter.

I cannot speak for today's kitchen staff, but at that time the fear that the computer would lose power whilst in the middle of a programme was one of our greatest dreads.

There was one occasion when I was working away like the proverbial beaver when the contents of the screen disappeared into a small dot at the centre of the screen. It was later established that a digger working outside the kitchen had struck the main electric cable, and that was a whole morning's work gone, like a glass of water thrown down the sink.

Warminster certainly had its fair share of visitors as this was the hub of the infanteers' wheel. If there was anything happening concerned with infantry, this was the place it was going to happen. I soon found myself working in the biggest Officer's Mess that I had ever seen, feeding some 120 officers on a daily basis, and this was just one of the three Officers' Messes in the establishment. There appeared to be a lunch for V.I.P.s almost every day, and it was my task to see that these 'top table lunches' made the standard that is required for such important clients. I expect that you, the reader, are saying at this stage, 'What client?' It is and always has been my idea that even if the person eating the meal is not paying, he or she is a customer that I would want back if it were my own business, and I still find that this makes the preparation of every meal that little bit easier.

The fact that the majority of these top tables were only for around ten people enabled me to experiment with new menus and ideas, and I think that was the most enjoyable part of the entire job. There are so many things that can be done with the hoards of foodstuffs that adorn the shelves of the usual Army kitchen and further afield. I have never forgotten the words of one of my first Cook Sergeants: 'Never be afraid to try something different,' – and this I believe applies to any chef or cook anywhere in the world.

This was an extremely interesting period of my career, and the fact that I was feeding some very interesting and important people has, I am sure, helped me to believe in myself as far as the small important dinner parties go. If there was no praise at the end of the meal from one or other of the guests then I had not performed to my best ability, or at least that was the way I looked at it.

It was during my posting to Warminster that I took up part-time employment as a taxi driver and this did help to keep up the standard of living that I had been accustomed to.

I would not of course say that there was a necessity for all soldiers to take up part-time employment, but the extra pocket money helped, especially when away from the family and with the need for two pockets to be kept filled. Not only that, but the job of driving a taxi was very flexible and therefore did not really interfere with the task of providing the hungry squaddie with his usual plate of chips or the like.

Warminster did however give me the greatest thrill that was possible, in my book at least. I was called into the office of the Catering Officer, Captain Dave Norris, and told that there was an exchange programme on the horizon, and would I be interested in applying for a place? When I enquired where exactly the exchange was, the answer that came bouncing back took me completely by surprise – 'Australia'.

Obviously, I had to consult my family, as this was not a particularly short trip, but one of five months. But I should have known that there was to be a selfless answer from my dear wife. 'You go,' she said, 'there may never be another chance,' so with that the very next day I applied. Of course, there was no doubt whatsoever in my mind that I would not be one of the 121 who were picked from the various corps and regiments throughout the British Army. I had applied for these expeditions before and been disappointed; and anyway I would not know for about three months. As time went on I forgot about life in the Antipodes and carried on with the life that I had become accustomed to, until the day that I was once again called into the office and the boss held his hand out and offered his congratulations. 'You are going to Australia!' he said.

To say I was flabbergasted would without a doubt be an understatement, and I replied to his announcement with obvious surprise. There was then the feeling of triumph at having beaten all the other candidates to join the other two Catering Corps ambassadors who were soon to be flying in the great Quantas Airlines Boeing 747 to the other side of the world.

My wife had, of course, got mixed feelings about the trip, and while on the one hand she was pleased that I should have achieved what I set out to do in the initial application, she was a little upset that she would not have the support that I would have normally been able to give her.

But to her credit she took it well and the decision did not cause too much trouble in the harmonic running of the family unit. After an agreement that I should write to her every single day, and vice versa, the planning and preparation was under way.

It seemed at first that no matter who I met or saw, all that I wanted to do was to make sure that everyone knew that I was going to the other side of the world, and for some strange reason it seemed to fill me with a great sense of achievement that I had been selected for this trip of monumental importance to me as an individual.

CHAPTER 7

The time between hearing the news and actually reporting to the air trooping centre at Brize Norton in the heart of the Oxfordshire countryside soon sped by, and as I climbed the cold metal steps into the RAF Tristar aircraft there was a great feeling of excitement and a buzz from the rest of the passengers, all of whom were travelling to the southern hemisphere on a four-month exchange that, although we had no idea at the time, would be more or less a paid holiday.

The feeling that filled the plane as we reached our first stop, in Singapore's Changi Airport, was exhilaration, and as we trooped from the plane all aboard noticed that we had been transferred from the gentle almost slow way that we in England go about our business to the extremely fast and bustling way that life lends itself to in the East.

After a short stop in Changi we were back on board for the final leg of the journey to Sydney. As I checked my watch I heard the by now familiar tones of the pilot informing us that we were now flying over Australia and, being the naive traveller that I was, I assumed that we were nearly at the capital of the Antipodes.

How wrong can a man be? I looked out of the window to see the brown sandy earth of the Nullarbor Plains, and believe me when I tell you this stretch of desert went on and on for hours, revealing to us just how big the continent of Australia is.

After the long flight we finally found ourselves circling over the famous Sydney Opera House, an awe-inspiring sight after the 24-hour flight that all on board had endured.

We touched down on the tarmac, and after the usual wait for clearance from the ground crew we disembarked and made our way through customs into the arrival lounge, to be welcomed by a group of Australian soldiers bearing the best gift possible, crates of the stuff that Australians wouldn't give a XXXX for.

After the initial briefing we were shown to the coach that, as army tradition would have it, was painted in the familiar dull green of all military vehicles. We then drove through the dark and into the Sydney suburbs to Liverpool, an outlying area of what was turning out to be a huge city, apparently the size of Wales.

Once we had been allocated our temporary accommodation for the night, we made our way to the canteen and soon realised that although a lot of the set-up was the same as the British kitchen, the food was certainly different. This became completely apparent at breakfast the next day when about a

third of the way along the servery there was a
container of stew that was the remainder of the
previous evening's meal. Of course, this was quite
acceptable for the Aussie squaddie, but I could see
the visiting soldiers avoiding that particular pot like
the plague, and I was no exception.

Apparently the way that the chefs there use up
the leftovers is to utilise it at the very next meal, and
it does not seem to matter whether it is breakfast,
lunch or dinner; if there is a pot of curry left from
that evening's meal, then it will be there to greet
your bleary eyes the first thing next morning.

Apart from that there is not a lot of difference
between the Australian army chefs and ours except
that they seem to be involved in a lot more duties
away from their trade such as guards and the like. In
England it is very unusual for chefs to do a guard
duty – of course, it does happen, but the chefs do
their own duties such as Duty Chef and all sorts of
functions that eat into their spare time, so they are
mostly excused the tedious task of standing under a
green poncho in the pouring rain checking I.D.
cards – a really important and vital job, but
burdensome nonetheless.

The hospitality that was shown to me on my visit
to Australia was second to none, and no matter
where I went it was always the same. I certainly
travelled a lot during that five months! I was
stationed in Brisbane, which is in Queensland and
just north of the famous Gold Coast, where even
the 'meter maids' (traffic wardens) are gorgeous
blondes wearing gold lamé suits. This area of

Australia is supposed to be the place where the 'beautiful people' live, work and play, and from what I saw this was definitely true.

The actual suburb of Brisbane that accommodated the unit, known as District Support Unit Brisbane, was Ennogera and was almost like something from the television soap opera. I soon settled into the somewhat laid-back and relaxed way that the folk there take life in general. I met up with a couple who were related to a friend of mine in Warminster, and the way they looked after me and accepted me into their family was incredible; they really made me feel at home, and I am glad that I enjoyed their friendship. I soon got used to the funny little phrases that the people in that country use, that at first were a mystery to me, such as when something was right they would say, 'She's apples,' in other words, 'That's good.' It became very apparent that whenever you saw a person that you knew you would ask, 'How are you?' whereas in England we only seem to ask that question on the initial meeting or at least not with the regularity that the Aussies did.

One of the few things that did take a lot of getting used to was the fact that they finished work at three. In the case of the senior ranks that was when the bar opened, and I soon found that I had to control the intake with more caution than I usually would have, because the heat out there seems to make the alcohol hit the brain quicker than it would back in dear old Blighty. I noticed that I was missing the evening meal and for that matter most of the evening, because by around six o'clock I was three sheets to the wind. This was a matter that desperately needed to be sorted out, because I was a lover of my food, and the obvious answer was easy – more practice! This option cured the problem but added another to the list of problems that plague us all during our lifetimes, and this one was definitely growing on me. I am, of course, talking about my weight and the fact that I put on another two stone during the five months' visit.

I was summoned to the Commanding Officer's Interview almost before I had time to unpack and was immediately posed the question, 'Where do you want to visit?' I had not been prepared for this question and obviously this showed. I mentioned that I had relatives whom I had never met on the West Coast north of Perth, in a small seaside town called Geraldton, but if that was not possible then I would welcome a trip anywhere. I was not to be let down as within a week I was off to Sydney again for a short stopover before flying north to the city of Darwin.

After a long flight I eventually landed at Darwin and was pleasantly surprised that it was nowhere near as densely populated as the big cities such as Sydney and Brisbane, and this place had an air of the olden days about it, very laid back and casual. I believe that this place is the home of some of the most beautiful sunsets that I have ever seen.

It was while I was staying at Darwin in the Sergeants' Mess that I made the acquaintance of a group of World War Two veterans on a reunion trip to the Northern Territories. I think the fact that I was a Pommie, and was more willing to listen to their war stories than the average Aussie, made me a popular centre point. Two days later I was invited to join them on a trip south into the bush to rediscover where they had last been together at the end of the war. On boarding the bus, it soon became apparent that apart from the driver I was by far the youngest member of the party, and I was 31.

Helping to relive the past

We travelled for hours through the vast desert and eventually pulled into an opening with a beautiful natural water hole. The trees around the side were abundant with fruit bats – there were thousands of them, and I had never seen anything to equal this.

After picking a fresh mango from the tree and allowing ourselves time to answer the calls of nature, we proceeded on our journey, passing a number of sandy hills that were the homes to who knows how many millions of ants, and the sight of cacti like one would see in the old western films was wonderful.

We eventually pulled into another clearing. I had noticed that the excitement and chatter amongst my fellow travellers was starting to get louder, and as the bus pulled to a stop and we disembarked I saw that the old comrades were now pointing excitedly to a sharp rise in the ground, and when I asked what was going on I was told that just over the hill was where they held their final camp. I was naturally used to the fact that in England if something is left undeveloped it is not too much time before a McDonalds or other such store is rising from the dirt to replace it. I thought that they might be raising their hopes if they expected anything to be there still. How wrong one can be. As we walked across the dam that held back a rather insignificant amount of water, one of the old boys told me that this was where they had held their final party before being sent back to their loved ones at the end of hostilities.

As we came through the bush there in front of us was the biggest pile of green beer bottles that I had ever seen, and these were still in good condition even though they had been sitting there for at least 45 years. 'The kitchen was over there,' I was told and, after a short walk, there in front of me in a slight hollow in the ground was the remains of a grease trap, still complete with the grease!

Obviously, the good weather in those parts had a lot to do with the preservation of the place, but it is an experience that I will never forget.

There were no buildings because these had been razed to the ground before the troops stationed there had left to return to their homes.

I learned a lot from the journey to the outback or bush with these old codgers, and one of the most important things that I felt, and that I would like to hold on to, was the comradeship. While I was in the Services I was always hearing from former soldiers who were now civilians that the only thing they really missed about the Army was the camaraderie, and now that I am one of the civilian band I feel that this is indeed true.

We arrived back at the mess and immediately indulged in a few bottles of the liquid gold and talked about the day's events, and I also had the time to examine the old lemonade bottle that I had picked up from the party site.

After a week at Darwin I flew direct to Melbourne and then on to the Australian Army Catering Corps' School of Catering at a small town near Melbourne called Puckapunyal, and here I saw for myself how similar it was to our own premises at Aldershot, only on a very much smaller scale. I even had the opportunity to teach a lesson and show how differently we in the British Army do things.

There was a lot of bar work done whilst I was in Australia, and it was done from the right side of the bar, namely the opposite side from the barman; and I suppose the fact that I increased my body weight by three stone or thereabouts proved that I enjoyed myself. Just for the record, it is a lot easier to gain the weight than lose it, as anyone who has ever tried will know.

It's a great life in the Army!

I finished my stint at Melbourne and flew back to Brisbane, where I took in the various tourist attractions such as the Gold Coast and Sea World, thanks to the courtesy of the friends that I had made, because without them I would have been slightly stuck for transport.

I did make friends with a couple who had emigrated from England whilst they were both still children and had met and married later in life, and when I enquired what they missed most about England the answer was two-fold: snow at

Christmas, and Caramac chocolate. Well, I could not do anything to help with the first memory, but that night I wrote to my wife to ask her to send a box of Caramac chocolate in the post next day. When it arrived the sight of this couple as they opened the box was like children with a new toy, and of course their own children just could not see what all the fuss was all about; but then if you have never had something you don't miss it, do you?

But this was the least I could have done for the family that had taken me into their home and treated me with the same friendship that a long lost relation would get, and I enjoyed my trip to Australia so much more because of people like this that I was glad to have something to give in return.

I also found that bar-b-ques in Australia are slightly different from those enjoyed in England, because whilst we cook immediately over the charcoal the Aussies have a solid plate with the heat under, and in effect acting like a griddle, but the final outcome is the same.

One of the best things that I saw whilst on that trip was in the parks and picnic areas; scattered all over these places were bar-b-ques, either run by wood or else electric, and if it was the former and you used the wood that was piled beside the barby then you simply went on a short walk and replaced it. If on the other hand it was electric, it was run by a coin meter, which gave enough power to cook the average family barby. All you had to do was clean it off when you had finished. I apologise beforehand if I upset anyone for thinking that English people would not treat this facility with the decency that is required to operate such a system.

After the trip to Brisbane I made another trip north to a place called Townsville, but this time on a bus. It was a long trip, and I stopped overnight in a small town with the name of Rockhampton, which is one of the centres of the cattle industry of this vast country, and certainly not as developed as the major cities.

Drinks on the mess balcony became a regular occurrence

From there I took the bus to Townsville. This was again a different type of municipality, and once more showed that the locals went about their life in a different way from those I had previously encountered. The pace had slowed right down and not in the way that we know a slow pace! This was a case of 'if it does not move it's probably asleep so be quiet or it will wake up'. It was during my time at Townsville that I was closest to the Great Barrier Reef, but at the time I could not really afford to visit it properly, so I did the next best thing and visited the Sealife Centre, where I actually walked through a glass tunnel amongst some of the deadliest sharks and other predators of the deep. I also managed to visit a tropical island called Magnetic Island; this was definitely the place to retire after a hard day's work and, as I sat at the pool side sipping the vividly coloured cocktail the waiter had just delivered with such finesse, my eyes drooped to a close and I fell into a light slumber, only to think of the wonderful way that life was treating me at present.

I returned to Brisbane and stayed for a few weeks before making the long journey from one side of the country to the other, eventually landing at Perth. Now this was a city and a half, and after spending two days wandering around discovering new and exciting things all the time, including a boat trip up the Swan River and a quick glimpse of the millionaire Alan Bond's house, I started the long drive northwards to the small seaside town of Geraldton to visit the relations that I had never even met. It certainly was a good evening and all too soon I had to make my way back to Brisbane for the final month or so of my visit. During the five months of living in the Area Sergeants' Mess at Enoggera I came to realise that, as in every English mess, they had their own traditions. In this mess all the residents were, as in England, known as the 'livers in'. But here they had their own little club called the 'RAT PACK' and after a short while I was asked to join, an honour in itself. Each member had a name to match his trade; for instance the RSM, who in this case was only an honorary rat because he did not live in the mess, was KING RAT. I gained the name of Bait Rat, because the chefs in the Aussie Army are always known as 'baitlayers'. This unique group had a meeting once a week to discuss who should be given the award for the biggest cock-up of the week and the winner, or should that be loser, had to wear a wooden medallion around his neck from the time he entered the mess to the time he left. If he failed, he would stand a round of drinks to all in the mess at the time. The word that was humbly engraved on the large medallion was RATFINK. It was also awarded to anyone who had caused a colleague to become embarrassed or otherwise harmed in any way.

Finally my 'holiday' was over. I can quite honestly say that during my stay I had every reason to like the people and the country of Australia.

When we returned to the shores of England it was the middle of winter, and didn't we know it! The snow was laying on the ground and England had been hit by one of the worst storms in its history.

I shall always remember that on my return everyone wanted to know all about the trip, and I thought that after four months of virtual holiday the task of returning to work would be rather tiresome, but there came a surprise that I was totally unprepared for. As I entered the boss's office he asked how I had got on and how everything was, and after I had stifled a yawn caused by the jetlag he told me that I had three weeks leave to take before April, so I had better go now. I walked out of that office wondering whether my life was being watched upon by some supreme being who obviously thought that I had had a tough life from 1971 till then, and so he was now selecting me for some further mark of his favour.

I stayed in Warminster for about six months after this trip and finally found out that I had been posted to the 1st Battalion, The Light Infantry in Omagh, yet another trip to Northern Ireland.

After travelling for the whole morning and catching an early flight to give us plenty of time to settle in to our new quarters, we landed in Belfast at Aldergrove Airport at around ten in the morning and I, being the leader of the family, had to find our contact who was to take us on the one-hour drive from Belfast to Omagh.

I expect that anyone who has not been in this situation would think that this was a bit cloak and dagger, but it is different out there. You just don't know who the enemy is, and on this particular day there was a great deal of tension. Let's face it, it is not hard to spot the average squaddie and his family. There was no one to meet us, and after several attempts to find out what was going on without giving the game away any more, I finally managed to get a phone call through to the camp and ask where my transport was. After a rather disturbing silence at the other end of the phone when I said that I was at the airport, the voice finally asked, 'Didn't you get the letter telling you that there was only one pick up?' That, it turned out, was after the last plane landed at 2100 hours, so here I was nearly 12 hours away from the time when the bus would pick us up. I did the best I could to protect my family, but all that consisted of was moving around the airport terminal every 20 minutes or so. After hours of waiting and fretting about how safe we really were I was finally able to find the bus or rather minibus, with the stress on the 'mini' part, because when we finally climbed aboard with about six other couples and baggage it was a less than comfortable journey to our new home. It had not been a good day and, as the Yale key turned in the lock we walked into what could only be described as a hovel! The place had not been cleaned, and it was freezing cold, even though the Corporal emphasised that he had switched the heating on for us. We later found that he had switched the heating on but he had not filled the boiler with coal, so the burner was happily burning away at the boiler with no fuel – I guess if the IRA did not get us this Corporal thought that he would have a go. But when you have had a day like that all you really want to do is sleep, and after throwing the bedding on the mattress that is exactly what we did.

After that initial welcome I settled down to my task and soon became part of the team which supplied the patrols with the meals that, as the old saying so well portrayed, kept them marching on their stomachs.

I had not been in the province long when I was sent to man a small kitchen on the border. The name of the place has slipped my memory, and for security's sake that is probably a good job. I stayed in this godforsaken hole for a week. We were in a solid steel hut with no light except the small rays that shone through when the door was opened. The task of trying to dress when you are in pitch darkness is difficult enough without the added difficulty of avoiding waking the men who have been on a particularly hairy patrol the previous night.

My stay there was disturbed by a phone call from the Families Officer who, without beating about the bush, informed me that my house was flooded and a replacement would be found when I could arrange it. The fact that my wife was visiting her parents in England (the usual thing for wives when husbands were doing their border stint) did not make the matter any better.

On return to my quarters I found the carpets quite happily drying over the wall outside the house and I am indebted to the man in the boiler house who allowed me to dry all the house carpets over the weekend. The cause of this watery catastrophe was a burst pipe in the loft that must have been running for a good day or so before the neighbours saw the water dripping from the upstairs windows and reported the fact.

After some time of tedious everyday routine

tasks, I was on weekend duty, and I woke earlier than usual and clicked the switch on the radio at the side of my bed to hear what every soldier in every unit in Northern Ireland dreads. A bus, full of soldiers returning from leave, had been hit by a bomb near Bally Gawley. I remember as clearly as if it were yesterday saying to my wife, 'That's our boys,' and I was right. I quickly got dressed and made my way to the cookhouse where I knew that there would be a mountain of bacon butties to be made in order to keep the nerve centre of the unit ticking over, because as always with this kind of disaster there are days – no, weeks – of work in order to clear everything away and ensure that everything that could be done is done.

I was standing behind the servery when a young Pay Corps Corporal approached with numerous scratches on his face, and I asked him what he had been doing. His reply took me by surprise: 'I was on the bus.' I did not expect any of them to be back in camp so quickly, so I wanted the ground to open up and swallow me. But he did not seemed too concerned as he sat down to a breakfast of bacon, eggs, sausage and all the trimmings. It was only later that I realised he did not even remember going into the kitchen let alone eating the breakfast – it's amazing what shock can do.

There were several changes to the ferrying of troops to and from the airport after that. I suppose some people would say 'a case of shutting the stable door after the horse has bolted'. The troops were taken to the airport at Aldergrove in Chinooks, those monstrous helicopters with the dual blades which, while I was in the province, had earned the nickname of Wokka Wokkas. I have no doubt that there are other names for them but for me and my family they were always known as 'the Wokkas'. I have never had the pleasure of a ride in a Chinook, but my daughter at the tender age of five had her first experience of a ride in this noisy flying machine and somehow managed to sleep for the entire journey – a feat that I will never understand, but I suppose she follows in her father's footsteps, because a squaddie seems to be able to sleep anywhere if the need arises.

Before moving to Omagh I had known that we were only to be in Northern Ireland for a year as the 1st Battalion of the Light Infantry were being posted en masse to Berlin to carry out the duties of patrolling the borders separating East Germany from this city which, through an agreement at the end of the Second World War, had been split into four zones. The British, French and Americans controlled the interests of the Western half, and the Russians the Eastern half.

In November the planning for the battalion's move was well under way, but now it was time to put the family's move into gear, and for Ann, my wife, and myself it meant a lot of planning. Firstly it was Ann's first posting abroad, and for me it meant the long drive from Ireland to Berlin via Devon to visit my parents. On arrival at Harwich we teamed up with two other parties from the battalion who were travelling on the same ferry across to

Hamburg. The crossing was one of the smoothest that I had ever had, and for one who is a renowned sufferer from sea sickness that was one hell of a relief.

After a quite short drive south we arrived at the Royal Military Police post at the mouth of what is known as the Corridor. This was a road linking the western half of the city to the rest of West Germany and after the drivers and heads of family had received a very intense briefing we entered the Corridor for the two-hour drive through East Germany.

This was a very daunting prospect, as in the briefing we had been told what to do if stopped by the Russians and another set of rules if stopped by the East Germans.

There was no easy way through this roadway. You must arrive at exactly the right time allocated to you; if you arrived too early you were done for speeding, and too late meant that you had stopped which was also forbidden, so all in all it was a harrowing experience and one that I only had to do twice, thank goodness. The Corridor no longer exists thanks to the end of the Cold War.

On arrival in the city of Berlin I followed the leader of the group off the Autobahn, which had in years gone by played host to the excitement of motor racing, into a large car park where the battalion had a representative waiting to meet us and guide us through the great maze of streets to our new home. A street with blocks of flats loomed up ahead with the peculiar name of Schmidtknobelsdorf

Strasse! Let's just hope I did not need to order a taxi to get me home after a skinful in the mess – I had trouble pronouncing it sober let alone in a stupor.

By this time, it was late in the evening and after a quick look around the new family home we made the bed and climbed into it. One of the most valuable things that I discovered in the many moves that I did all around the world was that the first thing you always did was to make the bed, because if you had a lot to do and were tired, if the bed was already made all you had to do was fall in.

This served as a very good answer to the ominous question, 'Where do we start?'

Next morning we started the task of documentation for myself and the family, things that up till now had not seemed urgent. But here we were in the centre of one of the most fascinating cities in the Western world, and the sooner we could get out and look around the better, although this being Ann's first visit to Germany there were difficulties with the language barrier. But in true traditional squaddie style I told her all she really needed to know was, 'Eine grosse Bier, bitte'; if she could master this, then I for one would be well catered for.

After the initial period of getting to know our way around and making new friends we settled into our new way of life and soon found our way around the city.

Driving proved to be a little on the hectic side and it did not take too long before you realised that the only one that you had to worry about was yourself because German drivers are renowned for not worrying about anyone but number one; it was a situation that I enjoyed, because it meant being on your toes from the moment you slammed the car door to the time when the key in the steering column turned anticlockwise and the engine goes silent.

We were living in the area of Spandau, which not many years before had been the place where the infamous Rudolf Hess was imprisoned; it was a relatively quiet part of the city. We made the most of the time that our posting to Berlin gave us and on many occasions took the opportunity to visit the Eastern part of the city, a journey that was just like something you would read in a thriller; after a briefing from the Royal Military Police at the famous Checkpoint Charlie, we moved slowly through the channel marked 'military vehicles'. All civilian occupants had to hold their identification papers up flat against the window of the car, which was locked shut, and during this time there was no communication between the Russian guards and the driver or the passengers at all. The driver, or the British soldier if he was a passenger, had to travel in uniform and therefore did not need to show I.D., but as soon as the guard had checked the number of occupants and logged them on his clipboard, we were waved through into what was like another world.

The depressing-looking buildings, which were, from a mixture of pollution and lack of funds, not kept up to the standard to which we are accustomed in our part of the world, were one of the first things that I noticed, but there were a lot of other things that revealed the poverty that was obviously rife behind the Iron Curtain.

Because I was in full uniform, I felt a little conspicuous and soon realised that we were, at some places, getting preferential treatment over the locals. This I presume was because the East Berliners knew that the average British soldier did not visit the East without a wallet full of the stuff that talks, and of course with an exchange rate of around ten East Marks to one of our Deutschmarks this meant that for £25.00 sterling, which was 100 Deutschmarks, we could reap around a 1000 East Marks, and believe me you could buy a hell of a lot for that sort of money!

Of course there is always a dark side to the story, because before leaving the West we were shown a list of what you could or could not purchase, but the British squaddie usually paid very little attention to this and took the risk of being searched by the RMP on the return journey.

On the occasion that my parents visited us in Berlin we visited the East and decided that we would go to one of the top hotels for lunch, and on arrival at the restaurant door were confronted by a queue of hungry East Germans waiting for a table. No sooner had we arrived than an eagle-eyed young waiter spotted my uniform and immediately grabbed me by the arm and as if by magic a table was found – it really made you feel a little guilty, but that was the power of money, and I guess that this was how the rich and famous on this side of what was the Iron

Curtain feel like, but perhaps without the guilt. We enjoyed a full three-course meal for the four adults and one child for around £5.00, not bad for one day.

On the return visit we always had the chance of being stopped and searched by the English Military Police, but never were, so I guess we were quite lucky in that respect. However, we decided right from the start that it would only have been considered greedy if we had flouted the rules, so we left the unpermitted goods in the East and returned with a boot-load of goodies, all of which are now scattered around the family home, and each is a reminder of the time we spent in Berlin.

Myself and Ann dressed to kill

There was always plenty to do in Berlin, and I suppose this is why we had our fair share of visitors. This was fine by us because it gave us the chance to show our families around this beautiful city, and it was during one of these visits that what was thought the impossible happened. My mother-in-law and sister-in-law had been with us for a week and it was the eve of their return to England when my sister-in-law decided that she had no photographs of the Brandenburg Gate and Checkpoint Charlie, so after our evening meal we embarked on the two-or-three-mile trip through the sparkling lights of the city. The traffic was, as always, heavy and after the usual stopping and starting we eventually arrived at the Brandenburg Gate and the necessary photos were taken. We then progressed to Checkpoint Charlie, where on arrival we parked in the usual carpark to the right of the wooden control box and right up against the wall. After a short walk we climbed the observation tower and I remarked on how mysteriously quiet it was and everyone agreed; usually this place was the buzzing centre for tourists and for those trying to get a glimpse of what they had left behind. I left that night wondering why it had been so quiet. The answer was evident when I switched the radio on the next morning, because between us leaving the checkpoint at around 7 pm and the present time of 7 am, the wall had collapsed and freedom had been granted to thousands of East Germans, and to put it mildly all hell had broken loose.

The next day the West German government agreed to pay a kind of bounty to all East Germans who required it, and because of this announcement banks the length and breadth of the city soon had queues a mile long at their doors.

What was already a heavily polluted atmosphere with the number of motor vehicles was about to be turned into a fog zone with the invasion of the two-stroke-engined Trabant, a car that resembled something that would have been favoured by Enid Blyton's Noddy, but that took the average East German years to save and pay for. The older models were said to have plywood bodies, but if this was the case then I never saw any such one.

This mammoth change in the course of world history gave me a slight problem as 99.9% of the world's press had now arrived in the city, and here I was with two relations over from England on standby return flights, with little or no chance of finding a seat in all this confusion. But after a lot of telephone calls the visitors were on their way home, and I am sure ever grateful to have been part of this momentous event.

The camp on the next day was buzzing as I returned from leave. It was the regiment's orders to set up tea stops at the various new openings in the wall, and to serve hot tea to any of the travellers, some of whom were at the end of an extremely harrowing journey and perhaps achieving a lifetime's dream. Within the first two or three days we had gone through several thousand pounds of sugar and hundreds of tins of the good old evaporated milk. But to see the faces of the people who crossed the border that day made the cold and wet quite bearable.

The entrepreneurs had already set up stalls selling small chunks of the wall and I myself managed to get a picture of my daughter, who at that time was only five, breaking into the wall with an axe, which I sent to my home town's paper in Devon, and they published it with a small story, much to the pride of her grandparents.

We of course collected numerous pieces of the wall because it did not take an honours degree in history to realise that this was indeed History in the Making. Small changes were already appearing in this remarkable city; what were once strict and stern East German or Russian guards delighted in having their photo taken with Lisa. It was very moving being able to watch the long-lost relatives wrapping their arms around each other, showing that the years of separation had not diminished the love that lies deep within the human frame.

It soon became quite the normal thing to see the Trabants putt-putting through the Spandau streets, and things that we had been able to buy cheaply in the East were now already being hit by the Western world's prices. There are ultimately always things that people need to do to prove to themselves, and write in their own history books, the facts as they remember them, and mine was to walk through the Brandenburg Gate, which of course these days is common practice but in that month of October 1989 was new, and one of the things that just had to be done.

It was one of the most remarkable periods of my life, and certainly one that still provokes a chill right up through the vertebrae whenever I think about it. But as with all things it was shortly to come to an end as far as my posting to Berlin was concerned. It was at the Christmas following the liberation of those poor unfortunate families in the East that I learned of my imminent departure from the city that had at least a thousand more stories to tell if I had only had the time to be told.

But it was during the annual kids' Christmas party that the Chief Clerk mentioned that he had received a posting order from records and that I was to be posted, but he could not remember where! Well, believe me, there is nothing worse than being told half a story, and now the magic of the party had been lost and would probably not be restored until I had found out the full details.

It was not until the next day that I discovered that I was bound for Essex and the garrison town of Colchester, supposedly the oldest market town in England. Well, as with all Army postings, it was a struggle to accept that the massive upheaval was yet again about to rear its ugly head.

There was however a brighter side to the story, namely promotion to the rank of Staff Sergeant; this indeed made the proposal a lot easier to swallow, and as we were in the bar of the mess at that time what better place to celebrate with a few jars of the liquid with the tall frothy head, otherwise known as German beer.

The packing started in earnest after Christmas, and even though this was the umpteenth time we had done it, it never seemed to get easier, in fact quite the contrary. Looking back, I suppose that we had become complacent about the amount of work that would be needed to present the married quarter back to the Army so that we had no bill raised against us for damage or for cleaning.

There was so much to do, and I don't think that the person who has never handed back a quarter realises just what is involved. Yes, of course there is a certain amount of personal pride, and let's be honest, no one wants rumours flying around that they left a dirty house behind them.

But when you have completed all the tasks that you feel were needed to finish, it is then time to start on the tasks that the Inspecting Officer would be looking for, and in most cases it would involve the dismantling of the cooker and cleaning until it is without even the most microscopic spot of grease or burnt-on remains of food. Next come the windows, and believe me when I tell you that I have tried loads of different 'tricks' to avoid the ultimate smears, but even so when the dreaded hour arrives for you to hand over the place the sun shines bright and shows more smears than were originally there. The mattresses were always a sore point, especially if you had small children. Inevitably we all have small accidents, and stains do not come out of mattresses that easily, I can assure you, but by listening to old soldiers in the past and applying a liberal dose of talcum powder you may well be able to disguise it. If you are not so lucky, you usually end up paying for the mattress, but of course the Army being the Army you do not get to keep the offending article so that this does not happen in the next house, and I am afraid that this was one rule that I never understood. It would have been a lot cheaper to issue a mattress for an individual to keep for his own rather than charge him a price that did not match the damage, but as I have already said that's the Army.

They had a lot of funny rules and by that I do not mean funny ha-ha but funny as in peculiar, and postings were no exception to the rule because, just when the family had settled into their new surroundings, the dreaded posting order would arrive on the Chief Clerk's desk and start the ball rolling for a whole new settling-in process. Some people, however, were fortunate enough to be granted an extension, but you had to be really lucky to be given such a stay of execution. This was to be my sixth posting, and just for once in my whole career I did not want to move, but with the prospect of promotion and more cash in the coffers how could you turn it down? Looking at the subject with hindsight, it would have been advantageous to say, 'No thank you, I would rather remain in Berlin.' But I didn't, and so here I was with time marching on and the sight of Colchester looming closer.

Of course, the journey that we had taken some 18

months previously was now being completely reversed but this time with the restrictions somewhat lifted. We arrived at the checkpoint ready to pick up our travel document, which was still printed in Russian, French and English. The journey still seemed to be just as nerve-racking, but there was another more pressing emergency that had been on our minds ever since we had received the posting order. We had only days before become the proud owners of a brand-spanking-new Toyota Corolla, something which most soldiers in Germany take advantage of especially as it is tax free and saves the buyer a couple of thousand pounds on the price one would pay in England. The problem now however was that if a soldier was posted back to England within a certain period the balance that was saved in the tax-free offer would have to be paid back. I can assure you that this sends a somewhat cold shiver up your spine. The question of how you are going to lay your hands on £1,800.00 is one with no easy answer.

The main problem was that even after obtaining letters from my Catering Officer and my Commanding Officer, and whoever else I could get to prove that I had bought the car in good faith not knowing that I would be posted, I would not know my fate until the ferry docked at Harwich, and, as I was told by the British Frontier Service in Berlin, it would very much depend on the mood of the Customs Officer on duty at that particular time. As we were docking at six o'clock in the morning this did very little to raise my optimism, I can assure you. The problem was that if the customs wanted money it had to be paid there and then or the car would be impounded, so I had to ensure that I had enough money in my account so that if the worst happened I and my family would not be stranded on Harwich docks without transport.

The crossing from Hamburg to Harwich was a good one, with only the faintest hint of a swell, and as we climbed back into the car and waited for the huge steel doors at the front of the ferry to open we knew that the moment that had caused us a fair bit of anguish over the last couple of years was finally here. As I engaged first gear the car crept towards English soil. I guided it in the direction of the red 'Anything to Declare' channel in customs. The gentleman on duty approached and asked the obligatory question, 'Anything to declare?' I asked if I could see someone about the car and was asked to park it and wait in a small Portakabin. I opened the door and despite the middle of winter the small Calor gas heater was pumping out all the heat that was required to make the hut rather cosy, although at the time cosiness was not what was ultimately on my mind.

I waited for a few minutes and the door opened, and a customs official entered. He beckoned me to sit down and said, 'What's the problem?', so I explained my predicament and showed him my array of letters, and he took at least 30 seconds to reply. 'OK, that is fine, but don't sell the car for at least 12 months or you will be responsible for paying the duty on it.' I sat waiting for the next part, but in fact once I had signed the forms required I walked back out into the chilly winter climate and sat back in the car and gave what is probably the loudest cheer possible. After I had explained to my wife she did the same.

The journey to Colchester is only a short one but after receiving this good, no, wonderful piece of news it made it the best short journey possible. We arrived on the Saturday morning and pulled into Gujerat Barracks to collect the keys for our new house. The kitchen was deserted, as it usually is on a weekend, and of course when you walk into a new environment in civilian dress no one actually knows who you are, but after introducing myself to the Corporal in charge of the kitchen I was passed the envelope containing the two keys to the new family home. I drove to the estate, and as with all new houses that you have not seen it was something of a blind date, not knowing exactly what the house was going to be like when we drove around the corner.

As it happened this one was, we found, not the best we had ever taken over by a long way, and the curtain that was to be seen hanging from the rail in the bedroom suggested to us that it was a disaster. On opening the front door we were proved to be correct.

But, as we had done many times before, we had our moan about how clean we had left the quarter in Berlin and then got on with making this the sort of home that we could welcome guests into without embarrassment.

Colchester proved to be a very busy kitchen with three units occupying the same space, but working well together as a team as, I am sure you are aware, we had all been trained to do. This meant that there were of course three Master Chefs all looking after their own units but with the Warrant Officer in charge overall.

After a year or so in this posting, the now well-known Saddam Hussein invaded Kuwait and my squadron was detailed to deploy to Germany to assist in the outload of 7th Armoured Brigade, the first units to be sent to Saudi Arabia to try and convince the dictator that he was wrong and should immediately withdraw his forces – which, of course, he did not. However, there was no cause for 1 Squadron to be concerned. We were definitely not going to the Gulf.

Now this seemed to be a familiar rumour and as with all rumours in the British Army you never know if it is true until either the danger is over or you are put on 48-hour standby and ready to move.

We arrived back in the UK around the September, if I remember, after four weeks' very hard and rewarding work and were once again told categorically that we were to be staying in England and not heading for the sandy climes of the Saudi desert. By the end of October the lorries had already started to be daubed in the sandy colours of camouflage needed to prevent them from being seen over the sand dunes. For a unit that was to be staying put it did not inspire much confidence. Then came the news that we had all been dreading – we were to move to Saudi early in the new year, and I am sure that I was not the only one who had the unenviable task of returning home that night to tell his wife the reverse of what he had told her some weeks earlier. There was the usual utter confusion, and as always the rumours were flying faster than the Tornados that were to be used so effectively in the war some months later.

Presentation of my Long Service/Good Conduct Medal
(15 years of undetected crime!)

CHAPTER 8

All the Senior Non-Commissioned Officers were allocated matters on which they were delegated to lecture the squadron, in order that the troops were updated on all they should know in the hostile desert that we were about to face. My prime area was Health and Hygiene, and I am sure that most of you reading this will be asking what this has to do with going to war, but it does have a great deal of importance because it involved items from how to recognise sun-stroke to how much water one had to drink in order to stop the astounding effects of dehydration. All these lectures had to be fitted within the pattern of the normal workload and that, for myself the same as for any other soldier, meant the days were becoming longer. This in itself was good training for the time the squadron was to spend away from our loved ones. On top of the day-to-day running of the catering operation within the barracks at Colchester there was also the preparation of the equipment that we would need in order to send the dreaded dictator fleeing back to Baghdad. The cookers that we were to take were the No.5 cookset, which consisted of a large metal suitcase which, when opened up and the four legs dropped from underneath, became a cooker of great suitability for mobile operations of this sort.

Of course, as with all things, inevitably there was to be a problem and, if the truth was known, many more after that one had been solved.

Now, whether or not the Army in its wisdom had suspected that before long something in the world would resemble what was about to happen I don't know, but it did seem rather coincidental that some few months before this had all blown up I had had to report to the Army School of Catering in Aldershot to learn how to convert these cookers to operate on the fuel that seemed to be most easily transported, petrol. This had indeed stood me in good stead for the training that I could pass on to my chefs, because although I myself was the Master Chef of the unit, my chefs would be split up into five locations, and each location had two chefs feeding an average of 120 men.

This therefore meant that we had a total of ten of these cookers, two for each field kitchen. It was agreed during the period leading up to the embarkation of our equipment – which incidentally preceded the men by some three or four weeks – that the second cooker would be kept on the truck and used for a standby or for spares. This proved to be a good decision as becomes clear later in this episode. This having been clarified I went through the procedures of lighting these monsters, which consisted of heating a tube within which was the petrol; this in turn vaporised the fuel and a fine mist was released which was then ignited and forced up to the burners, of which each cooker had four. If an oven was to be used it sat on top of two of the rings, and therefore only left two on which to cook. I am sure that there are some of you who are thinking that the practice of mixing petrol vapour and air and then throwing a match on it could prove dangerous. Well, you would not be wrong, but in truthfulness this really was a great piece of equipment and to be fair if used properly there was very little cause for concern.

Some of the benefits, and there were not many, of being in the catering department were firstly that you were always in the warm, secondly there was always something to eat and thirdly, especially in a transport squadron, you always had the same vehicle, which because of the code in the parts catalogue of field cooking utensils was called the G1098 wagon. These were very different from the normal four-ton truck, not in outer appearance but in the build and customisation that made them to all intents and purposes mobile kitchens, with shelving to carry food, and improvements such as a canopy that would swing out to make the walls and ceiling of the kitchen when stationary. Each troop had its own vehicle of this sort and they were made, we thought, to withstand the roughest of terrain. It was not until we were travelling over the sand dunes in the pitch black of night that we realised all our preparations had had no effect whatsoever, and we had to spend considerable time sorting out the various tins of rations, which when you consider that there are no labels on the tins, just the names printed on the top, was nothing but a nightmare.

The time passed rapidly and it was soon the morning that we were to depart for warmer climes. The conversation in the house seemed to be very minimal and extremely highly strung, because there was indeed an air of tension.

The final thing I did was to say farewell to my wife and daughter at the doorway to the kitchen and walk inside where I found a quiet corner in which I could shed my share of the tears that I knew my wife and daughter would at that moment also be shedding, and to this day the thought of it still brings a lump to my throat. It was probably the hardest thing I had ever had to do, and I would not want to go through it again.

Within a very short time we were climbing the polished aluminium steps of the coach that was to transport us to the midst of the Oxfordshire countryside and eventually to the departure hangar of Royal Air Force station Brize Norton. The gateman hoisted up the barrier and the bus made a slow, sedate entry into the camp. There was not a sound on the bus; no one had spoken all the way from Colchester. There was certainly a lot of thinking being done, that was evident. We all debussed and joined the several hundred people already assembled, and within minutes there was the usual distribution of 'next of kin' forms. Usually this had the effect of being slightly pessimistic but this time it was even more so. It was while this was going on, and I was standing near to my Unit Commander, when I overheard a remark which has been in my mind ever since. One of the more senior Private soldiers said to the Major, 'Do you realise, sir, that every man in this hangar has probably cried at some time in the last 24 hours?' and the Major to my surprise agreed. I had for some reason assumed that I was the only one who had released his tension through the tear ducts.

This had the sudden effect of making me realise that I was not alone, and that everyone in the huge drably painted hangar was, in the next 48 hours or so, about to face something that none of us had ever faced before: WAR. Of course at that time we none of us had any idea how the situation was going to end, and I was forever the optimist telling everyone that the politicians sitting around their long polished oak tables would sort it out long before we even had time to warm the vaporising tubes of the No.4 cookset. There were however a lot of men in my squadron who wanted nothing more than to have a bloody good scrap and return home to their loved ones in the same way as they left them, in one piece.

While we waited in the hangar we found as usual that we had literally hours to wait before we even saw the inside of the aircraft. This was the usual form in the Army and everywhere that we went you could hear the phrase, 'Hurry up and wait,' and looking back it certainly was a true-to-life saying.

Then one of the other Senior NCOs asked me if I fancied a pint. Well, I was not really in the mood but what the hell; with the drinking laws in Arab countries so vastly different from this country it probably wouldn't hurt to put away a few jars, purely for medicinal reasons you understand. The Sergeants' Mess was found in record time and the atmosphere was definitely lacking, but the beer was good, so what did it matter? Breakfast was served at around 5 am, and everyone tucked into a full English fry-up, bacon, eggs, sausage, beans and anything else that the stomach could hold. It was the best breakfast that I can remember while I was serving, and believe me, there had been some good ones.

After breakfast we were told to report back to the hangar where there were bodies lying everywhere. Troops had been arriving throughout the night and the place was now pretty full.

Soldiers are a rare breed, and if there is even the microscopic chance of there being a place in which the eyes could be allowed to close and grab an insignificant amount of sleep, the average squaddie will find it and utilise it to its full capacity. A soldier can sleep anywhere, and as his career carries on there are literally dozens of different situations where this becomes a very essential knack, from the old German pill-boxes on the island of Alderney to the cab of a JCB during a sandstorm in the Kuwaiti desert. Both these situations have been thrust upon me as a member of Her Majesty's Forces and as a member of the Army Catering Corps.

This was especially so because, as I previously mentioned in this journal, the cooks were always the first to rise and the last to get their heads down and take a glance at their eyelids from the inside.

However, on this occasion we were suddenly called, and before any of us had taken it in we were climbing the aluminium staircase that had been wheeled in to assist us in boarding the Boeing 747.

The jumbo was from the Kuwaiti National Airline and came fully equipped with pretty Kuwaiti air stewardesses who, as we entered the doors, handed out badges daubed with the slogan 'Free Kuwait'. As this was not completed with a question mark, I could only assume that it was a request! I immediately found myself thinking, 'As if we have a choice.' We took our seats, and it became obvious as the engines bellowed into life that there was, unlike the previous military flights I had endured, a sense of urgency. As the force of the huge Rolls Royce engines pushed us back into our seats and the wheels left the tarmac of the runway and, incidentally, British soil I felt myself try to swallow. It did not materialise, and a feeling of nausea overtook me from the very pit of my stomach to the top of my head.

We crossed various countries, all of which we could follow from the route plan shown continuously on the video screen during the flight.

I should like to be able to say that, as with most flights that I have had the pleasure to take, the feeling of nausea completely disappeared on touchdown, but this was no ordinary flight. None of us knew what exactly it was that we were to be faced with on arrival, therefore the feeling remained for at least the two days after landing and until I was actually doing the job that I had spent all those long years training for, and keeping up the motto of the Army Catering Corps, 'WE SUSTAIN.'

After a long haul of a flight we landed in the Saudi Arabian town of Al Jubail. I can honestly say that it was exciting, but still in the subconscious there was that gut feeling that we were here to take part in a war. My mind kept thinking back to the 1939-45 War and how long that lasted. Could we possibly be away from our families for that long? I, like most of us, hoped that it would still be settled amicably, but as the BBC Home Service reported, that was becoming less and less likely.

We were escorted from the jumbo and on to old rickety buses for the relatively short drive to a huge tented camp which, for reasons that were obvious, had a huge board outside the gates with these words 'Black Adder Camp'. We passed through the gates and were shown to our unit's accommodation, where we were greeted by the Squadron Sergeant Major, who had by now been in the location since before Christmas and had gained loads of valuable information. One of the first things that happened was the briefing which for once did not take long, and basically consisted of the camp rules.

It seemed unusual somehow, because at other times when we had been on exercise, it had only been a matter of hours before we were sniffing out the nearest pub and gaining reports on what the local talent was like. Here in Saudi alcohol was banned, and the talent were wrapped up so well in white sheets that the unwrapping seemed unthinkable. One of the first things that the SSM (Squadron Sergeant Major) showed us was the desert rose. I realise that you are by now thinking that perhaps this is some kind of poisonous flower native only to Saudi Arabia, but it had a much more important use, that of a portable urinal. The 'desert rose' consisted of a piece of two-inch plastic tubing that was inserted about three foot into the ground at an angle of around 45 degrees and with around the same measure sticking out of the ground into which was taped a large funnel. This had a very desirable effect of taking all the waste matter under the ground and therefore keeping the flying nuisances to a minimum. For those of us who needed to relieve ourselves in other ways the crappers were of a contemporary design and constructed of plywood into which was crafted a wooden seat with a 12" diameter hole on which you sat and released all your anguish. There is obviously something about toilet cubicles that attracts a very special subspecies of human being, that of Graffiti Artist. They are so widespread that even among a small handful of men in the middle of an area of land with nothing but sand for miles, the original works of art appear.

These consisted in Black Adder mainly of jibes from one unit about another, and only one really sticks in My mind and was written by a member of 15 Squadron RCT about 1 Squadron RCT and read, '1 Squadron is like a circus; it travels around, finds a nice spot, puts up its tents, lets out its animals and clowns for a while and then packs up and fucks off again,' and, although the 1 Squadron lads did not really appreciate it, myself included, it was to some degree true. But this applied to all the units that had deployed on Operation Granby – this was the name given to all the troops there in that godforsaken hellhole.

One of the first things that we were aware of on our arrival in Black Adder was the unbearable heat, and as usual our unit seemed to be the only ones without the cool desert combat clothing. Here we were dressed in the British combats, which just happened to be green in colour, and it does not take a genius to realise that there is not a lot of grass in the desert. Even the camouflage nets were green, but we were assured by our seniors that they still would have the desired effect when the eye of an Iraqi fighter pilot was scanning the ground trying to find a target. I can now tell you that the reassurance did not make me any happier.

If I shoot a camel, we can always stew it or mince it!

We had been on the ground a few hours and had found somewhere to get our heads down. I entered the huge tent and was confronted with two long rows of tubular-steel beds, some sporting snoring lumps of combat soldier and some loaded to the brim with Bergens (large rucksacks). There was no actual bedding as every man Jack had his own sleeping bag, and it did not really matter which empty bed frame and mattress you took because there was no doubt that you would only be there a matter of hours before you would be moved to the next location. It was true this time as well as any other; after a briefing with the troop commanders we had been told to expect to move out during the night.

No one knew exactly where to, or what our first location would be like, and after driving for some considerable time the convoy came to a halt. There was no need to erect the canvas that night, and the best thing for everyone was to get as much shut-eye as was humanly possible. I had my own duties to sort out, like finding out exactly what time the O.C. wanted the men to eat breakfast. After I had found this information, I then had to pass it on to the eight chefs under my command; that way the whole squadron would be working the same pattern. From what I remember after crawling into my sleeping bag it took one hell of a long time to get warm, and by the time I did reveille reared its ugly head. Daylight was just breaking and now the work would start in earnest, to erect the 12-foot-by-12-foot tent that was to become our kitchen. This had been modernised to fit as a lean-to on the side of the four-tonne Bedford truck, using the back of the truck as a store as well as it doubling up as the chefs' sleeping accommodation. The cooker, if you can call it that – I prefer to call it a cookset – was dragged from the side of the truck and petrol was soon seeping into the small tin well that was used as the source of ignition for the pre-burner. This was the big test, but the main burners were soon lit and all four blazed with what was soon to become a familiar glow.

Fast food – Open All Hours Gulf-style

I suppose that I should consider myself lucky because had we been there five or six years earlier I would have been returning with biceps like Arnold Schwartzenegger, because the old No.1 burners had pressure pumped into them by a hand pump and were a lot more work than the foot pumps that we had by then.

Within minutes of life being aroused in the burners I had two six-gallon containers of water on to boil. One of these was for the urn of tea, and the other was to go into the large green Norwegian flasks that held enough water for a good forty to fifty cups of tea. These were known affectionately as 'noggies'; it is quite humorous how in this sort of environment things as simple as a flask gain an almost friendly identity.

The sausages were soon frying nicely on the top of the oven vent, which was still hot enough to cook on but not hot enough to burn it. There is a captivating little phrase that is probably well known to every Army chef, 'When it's brown it's cooked but when it's black it's fucked,' and believe me there has never been a truer word spoken. There is very little food that can be transformed from the black sorry state that you may discover still in the oven back to the delicious golden brown that it would have been if you had discovered it about ten or fifteen minutes earlier.

Before long the queue started to form outside, and it became apparent that the fact that all of us had been away for just over 48 hours had not spoiled our appetites. As the queue of about 80 men slowly wound its way past the six-foot wooden trestle table I realised that I would soon be able to identify all the men in my troop by the different mugs, and I don't mean the ones on their shoulders. There were china ones, plastic of all colours and even the old white enamel with the blue rim.

If there is one thing that a chef soon gets to know in this sort of location it is his customers. They are, I suppose, a captive audience and quite apart from the odd, 'I've just popped in, is there a brew on?' we saw them all for three meals a day, except of course where they were on night duty, and I think that this was the only time when any man would miss one of the three meals served to the unit throughout the day.

There is no doubt about it that breakfast never provided us as chefs with the problems of menu planning that the other two meals did. It is quite acceptable to have bacon and eggs for every breakfast for six months, but if you put cottage pie on for lunch every day there would soon be a lynching party ready to hang you from the nearest set of makeshift gallows.

When on a giant exercise of this kind you had very little control over exactly what rations were going to be delivered to the unit, and if you got something a little out of the ordinary then it was usually kept until it could be used to its best advantages. The Squadron Quarter Master Sergeant (SQMS), who is basically in charge of anything that requires storage, is in wartime responsible for the ordering of food, and this is very simply based on the number of men in your unit. He will put in a demand for a number of rations and then the Royal Army Ordnance Corps will put together a huge package of what they think the unit would need. Now this really takes a lot of consideration, and at the first thought one would think that the Master Chefs of the units would be the best people qualified to decide what exactly their troops require to cover them for the three days before the next pickup rendezvous.

War was new to the vast majority of us. There were a few who had made it to the Falklands and more thankfully made it back, but none of them were among my happy band of chefs. That night the rations arrived and the SQMS came in for his cuppa and said to me, 'YOUR Rations are on the back of the wagon.' After a few minutes, and after delegating two men to assist me sort the rations into the four locations I made my way to the parked four-tonne truck, and in the pitch black of night I climbed aboard. The beams from our torches were darting about all over the back of the interior of the canvas-clad vehicle. In a matter of moments there was a bit of excitement; one thing that none of us realised was that driving through the desert in the pitch black without lights and relying totally on navigation by map and stars is not the easiest thing in the world, and when a drop over a dune of around 20 foot is not expected it does throw the contents of the back of a truck around slightly – well, more than slightly, it practically destroys any semblance of normal storage! The stores looked as though they had been emptied from a huge bucket and cascaded down in no particular order.

This had to be sorted in order to reach my troop locations by morning ready for lunch the next day, which meant that it had to be sorted in the dark, and since at this point the war had not started, no one gave any consideration to light restrictions. However, the Officer Commanding had his own ideas and why shouldn't he? That was why he was being paid a salary that made mine look like chicken feed.

He poked his head in through the canvas and in the tradition of the '39-'45 Air Raid Warden said, 'Turn that fucking light out!' Silence and darkness fell in the truck and I remember thinking, 'How am I meant to sort this lot out in the dark?' But we did, and I made sure from that point that each location spread out their rations to make them last until we could sort out the next batch of rations in the daylight. But it soon became evident that the RAOC did not know that our unit had split into four locations, or exactly what it was that we required to keep our lads fed well enough to supply the ammunition to the artillery on the front line. This was probably, for example, why at first they kept sending me whole gammons which if the unit were all in one location I could have cooked whole and sliced, but trying to split a gammon into four so that everyone got a share was practically impossible. It stood out quite clearly that the supplies we were receiving from the ordnance depot did not reflect exactly what the unit requirement was, which is probably why I personally buried around a hundred bottles of Robinson's Orange Squash somewhere in the Saudi Desert. This, I can assure you, was not done because no one was drinking it but simply because we could not carry it. There just was not the room, so it had to be ditched, and from reports from other Master Chefs who I met during the conflict this was indeed a common problem. If the chefs had been allowed to ask for specific rations the waste factor would have been considerably reduced. I am glad in hindsight that I did not have to calculate the wastage from this breakdown in the system, because if it could have been calculated then it would have run into many thousands of pounds.

There was an ever-increasing market for the American troops' meals, otherwise known as MREs or 'Meals Ready to Eat' and consisting of various menus, all sealed in dark brown foil-like pouches, which could either be opened and eaten cold or boiled in the bag until hot and steaming and producing the kind of odour that the Bisto kids would have been proud of; but of course whilst the British squaddie wanted the Yank meals the Yank soldiers wanted our compo rations. For those of you who have never had the pleasure of eating 'hard tack' biscuits or enjoyed the delicate taste of 'cheese possessed', or should that be processed, let me take you on a short but knowledgeable tour of the 'compo' or composite ration box. This was packed in a brown cardboard box and sealed by two metal or plastic bands.

Once opened the box contained an Aladdin's cave of goodies. This particular ration pack was a ten-man one; this was scientifically formulated to produce the correct balance of diet for ten men for a 24-hour period or five men for 48 hours or any other permutation of the original. Once inside there was a good display of brass-coloured tins with the familiar black printing that told us the chefs, or indeed the soldiers who were using the ration pack, exactly what we were to be cooking that day. Along with the tins were the other necessities that a soldier needed to survive the 24 hours. There was always a small polythene bag in which were neatly packed a menu sheet, with various ideas on how to cook the contents, along with a small metal tin opener. One of the other items in this pouch was around 20 sheets of toilet paper and, although this was considered essential, none of us ever used it; the average soldier always took a roll of the nice soft stuff even if it did have a rather feminine pink colour to it.

Compo rations are designed to be eaten cold and there are various menus which include such things as pilchards in tomato sauce. Of course I can hear you thinking UGH!, and I would like to be able to tell you that the roughie toughie squaddie liked nothing better, but I would be lying. So, the intrepid chef would mash some fresh potatoes if they were available and swiftly make them into fish cakes.

What's the recipe today, Jim?

A great deal of the contents had their own identification in the way of pet names; to give you an example steak and kidney pudding was known as 'babies' heads' because when they were taken from the tin the pastry that surrounded the meat was smooth and resembled to the inexpert eye 'skin' and of course once the skin was broken the insides were supposed to represent the brains. This I know sounds macabre, but if you ask any squaddie who has served in the field they would be able to tell you immediately what a baby's head was. This, incidentally, was the soldiers' favourite dish out of the seven or eight menus available, but of course the chefs, who knew about good food, would have found it pretty boring if they had had the same menu.

Therefore, we chefs had to make the most out of the hard situation that we could not order exactly which menus we would have delivered. I had tried a lot of different ways to serve babies' heads, such as savoury beef crumble. This was simply a case of removing the top layer of pastry and replacing it with a mixture of flour, margarine and cheese, which of course is mostly the same ingredients as pastry, but sprinkled onto the top and baked until crunchy this gave a totally different appearance to the dish, and the majority of the soldiers enjoyed the change. Another of my own favourites was to make the corned beef that was supplied with one of the other menus into hot pot. Believe me, when you are cooking meals that are served three times a day over a period of three months with the same ingredients, there has got to be a certain amount of ingenuity involved. Of course, there was a great part of the rations that, although included in every box, it was almost impossible to get the customer to eat. I am talking primarily about the small tins of processed cheese (otherwise known as 'cheese possessed', you remember), and while there were the select few who would enjoy the solid yellow mass that was being

197

pushed out of the top of the tin by half-opening the bottom, the majority of the tins got thrown onto the fire. I suppose, looking back, that this could have had quite dangerous results; as the tins had not been punctured they had a tendency to explode and go flying past your ear at about 90 mph and squealing like a wounded pig.

This was a regular daily occurrence simply because we could not get rid of what was over. Once we had grated what we needed for the cheese flan or whatever else happened to be on the menu that day, the rest had to go, and into the fire hole it went.

At first when we arrived in the desert there was not a lot of work to occupy the men in the troop, so they took out their frustrations in digging the deepest holes that I have ever seen dug by hand, but this was in fact extremely therapeutic, because one of the most important things is not to let the lads get bored; indeed at one location two of the boys designed and built an ornamental garden using the sand bags and any other bits and pieces they could find. Of course, for the chefs the lifestyle was a little more busy, but if we organised ourselves properly there was still the time to enjoy the lull before the storm, and remember that at that particular moment we did not know if there was going to be a storm.

Since returning from the Gulf it has become very apparent that all of our families back home knew more about what was happening than we did. All that we could rely on in our location was the

American Forces Radio, and that was a little vague, but at around 2200 hours each evening there was a full military briefing style programme which was supposed to tell us exactly what had happened during that particular day. The daily influx of mail helped, but it was usually three days old and therefore old news but believe me I was extremely surprised and pleased at all the support that we received from back in good old England. We were receiving sackfuls of letters from people we did not even know and gifts from people who, although they did not know you, they 'knew your mother'. It was astonishing; there were cakes from bakeries back in Colchester and hundreds upon hundreds of letters from young single females who were just happy to give the boys someone different to write home to, and at times promises of just what they could expect to receive when they did get home. But the truth of the matter is that no matter what kind of letter it was that had your name on the envelope it was a welcome sight, unless of course it was the dreaded 'bank statement' because that told us exactly what our better halves were spending back home; but believe me, we did not really worry about that too much.

Relatives that I had not heard from in years were now writing to me, and this did not make me in any way resentful – it was a warming feeling to know that so much of the country was behind us in this way. It really made the days a lot more acceptable.

Another pastime that could also have been a life-saving exercise was to dig what was known as a 'shell scrape'. I could not understand why it had been given this name unless, of course, it was to get you out of a scrape when the shells were landing all around.

We stayed put for a reasonably long period to start with, and when the air war started we would regularly stop what we were doing to watch the B52s crossing the sky to drop another deadly load on the strategically plotted targets in Iraq. They were so high up it really did take a good focused eye to see them, but they gave me, and I think all the troops on the ground, the ego boost that we needed, and that helped to make the allied troops the fighting force that the final achievement confirmed.

The food that was being served became more and more of the kind that could be kept hot, because it was getting to a situation where we, the men on the ground, did not even know if the land war was going to happen or not. If it did, we would have to be ready to move at a moment's notice, and believe me it wasn't just a case of sitting in a Land Rover and screeching away like the movies would have you believe. There were tents to be dismantled and put onto the trucks, food to be cooked ready for the move just in case there was not time to stop and cook, or in case of darkness falling so that we could not light up the burners for fear that the enemy would catch sight of the flames. It was not long before the ground war was obviously imminent, and I for one was still hoping that it was never going to come to the full-blown war that had threatened, but on the eve of the start of it all I cried. It had been a good many years since I had had this sort of tears in my eyes, but they were present then, and I am still not sure to this day whether they were from fear or just the fact that I still had not expected to be at war during my long career. I am not ashamed of the fact that I cried that evening; I am sure that there were a lot of others in the same boat as myself and more than likely with the same emotions, but of course we all kept it a secret from each other.

That night on the American Forces Radio we all heard for ourselves that the land war was under way and I started to prepare the catering side of the squadron for the move in Iraq.

There is a certain belief that the desert is lovely, and to some extent this is true, but when you are moving through the night with stores packed to the ceiling in the back of the truck and you hit a sand dune and basically fall down the other side, you begin to wonder. It does tend to throw all the stores around somewhat, so on reaching your destination it was a requirement to reassemble what had been, at the start of the journey, a reasonably tidy stores truck. It was with some trepidation that we proceeded in the direction of Iraq and even more so when the convoy ground to a halt and each vehicle in turn received orders from an American dispatch rider. The truck in front of us pulled away through an area marked with orange tape, and as my truck window drew level with the dispatch rider he very calmly told us to keep to the tracks as we were about to enter a minefield! It would be true to inform you at this stage that this was definitely not the best time to have two suits on, because there was no way a quick release of the trousers could be executed. We drove at what can only be described as a careful pace through the 100 yards or so. I suppose everyone was waiting for the bang, but as I am here writing this you will no doubt have guessed this did not materialise.

After a few miles and a lot of hours later we arrived at a huge mound of sand that had been built by the Iraqis in order to stop the Coalition forces from entering their beloved country. This by now had been proved a worthless task as the Americans had already cut through the mound, and a huge sign had been erected in true American style reading 'Welcome to Iraq Courtesy of The Big Red One'. This was the name for the American 1st Infantry Brigade who had cut the swathe in the mound in order to give us access into the barren land that lay before us.

We set up camp, as it were, on the top of what looked like a large hill but in actual fact was just another mound. We started to produce the best meal that we could, but because of the restrictions on lights we could only manage biscuits, cheese and luncheon meat. There were the obvious moans and groans, but this was not a decision that could be altered. There was a silence in the air that became slightly eerie as we dossed around waiting for the next move. It was now starting to turn darker. I remember the next thing as if it were yesterday. I was lying in the back of the truck when the sky was lit up by trails of vapour coming from the tails of rockets and then within a few minutes the loud but dull thuds as they hit the ground around the enemy locations. This bombardment was incredible and, no matter what the experts say, being on the receiving end of this must have been slightly more than just demoralising. The fusillade stopped after around 15 minutes and the air became silent again, and when my heart had stopped pounding I drifted off into a restless sleep. It was about 4 am that the second barrage went overhead and this one was a lot louder and a lot more intense. I remember saying to a colleague that I actually pitied anyone on the receiving end of that lot; it was incredible and knocked spots off any firework display. It was a little unnerving because here we were, some 150 men standing in the middle of the desert with the MLRS (MULTI LAUNCH ROCKET SYSTEMS) searing overhead and there was absolutely nothing being sent in our direction – we were just standing there cheering.

It was very evident that the Coalition forces meant business and I was extremely glad at that moment that it was that particular side that I was on; there had been times leading up to the war that I was not so sure! It is one thing knowing that within weeks you are going to be in Iraq facing a hostile force, but when you read in the papers just how large that force is and how relatively small our own Army is, it makes you sit up and wonder just who exactly is in the best position to win the bloody war.

I did find that I was going out of my way to attend any church services that were organised and I found a great deal of comfort in the fact that God was with us; even though I cannot really consider myself to be that religious, it made me feel that little bit more secure, and I suppose that it must have been the same for a lot of my companions, as there was always a good attendance at these services and a great deal of trouble had been taken in setting the mood, as it were. In one instance there were two tanks placed with their guns protruding into the air and almost touching, forming a kind of arch, and the makeshift pulpit was placed in between the two making a good background for a church service in wartime.

There was no time during the build-up to what was now happening that I was not just a little bit scared, and this made the task of getting on with what I had to do even more important in order to keep my mind off this feeling inside of me.

We eventually started the drive from the edge of Iraq across country and into Kuwait. It was dark by now and as we travelled along at the slow pace which had now become the norm, a sight greeted us that none of us had expected. We were caught slap bang in the middle of what seemed to us like a massive gun battle, and the tracer fire was going overhead. It was as spectacular as the fireworks at the Last Night of the Proms, but without the tune of Elgar's Pomp and Circumstance March. It all of a sudden made me realise that this was it, here I was in the middle of the war and I didn't have a clue where we were, or for that matter where we were going. After a while the tracer eased off and the convoy drew to a halt. I leapt from the wagon and took up a position that I considered safe, whilst I could hear the gunfire of our own artillery, whose ammunition we were carrying, blasting away in the distance.

It was at this time that I saw the Company Commander coming towards me and, I suppose rather stupidly, I asked, 'What is going on, sir!' to which he replied whilst drawing a small map in the sand with a stick, 'We are here, and the Iraqis are here, here and here,' pointing at the map with his weapon; 'If ever there was a good time to pray, this is it,' and he then proceeded to walk away. I stood there for a few minutes and pondered on what he had meant by it but then I decided that if I was going to get killed that was that and, believe me, there is not a lot one can do about it in this situation.

It was extremely hot in the middle of the desert and this was not helped by the fact that we had to be wearing our NBC suits on top of our normal clothes, so perspiration was indeed present.

What a shower!

During the next day we stopped and dismounted from our vehicles and dug in. One of the first things that you do in wartime when a vehicle pulls to a halt for any length of time is to dig a shell scrape. This means that a trench, about 12" deep and as long as your body, is dug in order to keep your body below the lie of the ground should there be shells landing around you. This I suppose protects you from the blast as the shells land. After digging in I decided to sit firm for a while; then I had a decision to make. Nature had called on me to rid my body of its normal waste. Not a problem normally, but this was wartime and I still had to undress from the two suits that adorned my body, not to mention the risk that was involved should we be attacked. But God was on my side, and as if by request a violent sandstorm blew up. I thought that this was as good a time as any to take advantage of the situation, and positioned myself over the A-frame that was between the four- tonne truck and the JCB, and did the business. I can almost hear the non-soldier types among you saying how in the hell could anyone have a crap like that and in the open as well. Let me tell you, if you have to go you have to go, and it will always be at the worst possible time, and this could not have been much worse.

After the best crap for quite a while, the sandstorm was now easing, and news was just beginning to creep in from Kuwait City that the Coalition forces had retaken the city and the war was practically won. Of course, no one was quite sure whether this was a true statement or had come via rumour control; as anyone with an ounce of common sense will tell you, it does not take long for a rumour to start. A statement overheard is enough to start it off and invariably the statement is always heard wrong anyway.

This seemed like a good time to serve up the stew that was being kept warm in the Norwegian containers, which did the job admirably. The queue started to form and before long the hot steaming brown mass was falling into mess tins and being scoffed down as quick as was possible before we had to pack up and move on to the next location, which was indeed Kuwait City. As the convoy moved slowly under the murky smoke-ridden skies, over to the left we noticed a huge crowd heading our way and as we passed by we noticed that they were Iraqi soldiers who had been taken prisoner and were now walking with their hands raised above their heads and were, to say the least, looking pretty sorry for themselves. It was hard not to feel sorry for them oneself, unless of course you were the type of person who could put their emotions behind them, and I was not built that way. Of course, a few weeks earlier I had been receiving jab after jab in order to protect me from the chemicals that the Iraqi leader had proposed to use during the 'mother of all battles'. The tablet that I took every eight hours in order to protect me from any nerve agent that he or his army may have used against us was, quite honestly, a pain in the ass, and indeed there were the odd few who had decided not to bother taking them because if they were going to be hit by this extremely obnoxious substance then they did not want to be around afterwards. During our NBC training we had all seen pictures of casualties during the Vietnam War that had been hit by mustard gas and blister agents, but my particular way of thinking was that if we had the best equipment in the world then we did not have a lot to worry about and, as our NBC suits were selling on the black market for around £200.00 to the Yanks and anyone else who would buy them, we must have been well equipped. There was of course no way in the world that I would have sold mine; it was to my mind the most important protection.

We arrived in Kuwait City and set up the troop location, and all the rigmarole of digging in started all over again, but now hopes were raised; it looked very much like it could all be over very shortly and we would all be able to go home. I assured myself that this would not be for months if I knew the British Army; nothing was ever that simple. Even if the war was finished there would still be the clean-up operation. The best thing that I could do was to go on feeding the men to the best of my ability and do my bit in keeping morale to its present high level. Within hours, literally, of the rumour reaching us it was confirmed that the Iraqis had surrendered and the war was won. Already there were to my surprise feelings of unease that we were not going all the way into Baghdad and destroying the dictator completely. I myself, maybe through a general feeling of fear, was pleased that it was over and that was that, but a great many colleagues wanted blood, and it showed in their emotions that this was what they had come over here for and it had now been stolen from right under their noses.

During the period that followed we made every effort to occupy ourselves with activities. I managed to get hold of one of the military motorcycles and ride it around the location, which was extremely therapeutic as I had always enjoyed motorcycles. Some just managed to relax by sleeping, and others actually volunteered to assist in the kitchen but that did not last too long in the heat of close to 150 degrees Fahrenheit.

During our time in Kuwait we amassed a great deal of rations that just could not be used, such as Robinson's Orange Juice, and it was felt that this should be donated to the local hospital. I delivered it with a few colleagues and it was gratefully accepted. I did manage to get out of the camp location and have a drive around in the back of a Land Rover, where we came across an Iraqi command post and, looking at how well they were dug in it was a miracle that we were where we were so quickly. There in front of us was a whole Portakabin that had literally been dropped into a huge hole and the surround filled in with the remainder of the sand, and a flight of rough and ready steps leading into the front door If this was not a well-protected environment for the officers to run their armies then I don't know what is.

However having said this, it was a pity for the conscripts that the Iraqi Army was mostly made up of that they had to suffer such inhumane conditions. At one point we came across an Iraqi food store, and the contents were amazingly enough all one commodity, rice. It must have been pure hell for the young soldiers who had been forced into this war and really did not want to be there at all, let alone eat rice for God knows how long.

It did not take long to achieve the ultimate goal and after three days of constant movement and driving the war was over. Now came the problem of the rumours about just when we would be able to go home. Everyone knew that it would take a long time to clear up, and it would be a fair while before we moved in the direction of Europe and ultimately home. We eventually uprooted ourselves from the location just north of Kuwait City, and moved down the road leading to Basra. This was lined with vehicles that had literally been blown to smithereens by the Coalition air forces, and now had been pushed to the side by the huge tracked vehicles of the U.S. and British forces to make a thoroughfare for the victorious troops.

We eventually left that road and headed for Saudi Arabia. It was whilst on this journey that we came into contact with the huge oil-well fires that had been lit by Saddam Hussein's army as part of his strategy to win the war. The air was thick with the billowing smoke, and probably highly toxic if the truth was known, but there was no doubt that the heat that these fires were giving off was immense. We were around half a mile away from the actual well but could still feel the heat from the inferno. The air around the whole location was a mustardy colour and once again seemed to make everything muffled in its sound, and the acoustics would have been a sound engineer's nightmare. The nearer we came to the oil-well fires the hotter it got, and the thicker the atmosphere, but eventually we came out the other side and arrived at a staging post set up to give the retiring troops a feed on their way back to Saudi. This was for us chefs a time to meet up with a number of our own corps who, through no fault of their own, had been delegated to set up this 24-hour kitchen to feed the thousands of soldiers of many races who had put the dreaded dictator to flight.

The Bedrock Café

After a really good meal, that always tastes better when cooked by someone else, we re-boarded our vehicles and departed for the next squadron location, which turned out to be just off the main road back to Al Jubail and was in the remains of an old quarry. My troop's kitchen was located directly under a huge piece of iron that was holding back a colossal amount of stone and old reinforced steel. At first I thought that it was not a particularly good place to set up, but a second look told me that by the amount of rust that was on the huge steel construction, this particular fabrication had been there for a great number of years and if it had been going to fall it would have done so by now . This was, I suppose, for me the best location of the lot and whether that was because the war and hostilities were over and we were working in a more relaxed atmosphere is still a question that I cannot answer, but once again within an hour or so of setting up the tentage the burners were roaring into action and the familiar shape of the pressure container was perched on the top ready to make the first cup of tea for the weary drivers and their crews, to revive the taste buds. There now began the task for the drivers of bringing back equipment from the front line, and returning the items to the various ports ready to ship out and back home. It was at this time that I managed to get a trip down to Al Jubail; I knew that there was a Warrant Officer who was in one of the camps from whom I might well be able to scrounge a few luxuries that those who had been in the thick of it, as it were, had not been able to obtain. Here they were with, relative to us, all the comforts of home such as a proper dining room, TV rooms and videos and a much wider choice of commodities with which to cook. I found him and posed the question, 'Got any gissits?' (A 'gissit' was the term used for anything that had been given, since people would identify exactly what it was that they wanted then approached the owner and say 'Gissit' or 'Give us it'.) However, he looked at me and shook his head. He was not going to help me out in any way, shape or form, and I found this absolutely unbelievable! They must have known what we had had to put up with for the last two and a half months. So we went back empty handed.

It took a lot to believe that the esprit de corps had not come up trumps, but this time there was no doubt I had failed in my attempt to secure extra stocks. A quick thought passed through my mind that I was glad I had not been the scrounger in Colditz, as this might have meant the failure in an escape attempt.

There were now opportunities to relax a little, and I spent a little bit of time riding the motorbikes over the paths that had been carved by the stone workers in the quarry when it had been used many years ago. Then within days came the news that we had been waiting for: the return home! It was, quite obviously, the best news that we had had for a good while, and it was not long before we were moving in that familiar convoy that had formed part of the victorious Coalition a few weeks previously on the road to Al Jubail. After an uneventful but nonetheless exciting drive of around two hours, we finally arrived at the luxurious end of the war zone with, wait for it, proper beds! We had not had this experience for a long time. After dumping our gear in the bedspace that we were to occupy during our short wait for a flight home, we had the task of taking all the vehicles to the port ready to be shipped back to the UK. While I was lounging across the bonnet of the Land Rover and soaking the sunshine, up bounced the Sergeant Major. Here we go, I thought, but gone was the attitude of the typical SSM and in was the Human Being. This was confirmation indeed that the war was over, especially as the question that he posed was to give me the chance of a lifetime. 'Do you want to come with me to Bahrain?' he said, and of course after being slightly taken aback I gave him a positive response, and within minutes we were on the road to Bahrain with another Staff Sergeant, Bud Slaney. After a drive of around three hours we saw in the distance a very long and quite dramatic causeway leading from the Saudi mainland into the state of Bahrain where alcohol is sold, in a quantity that is, after three months without touching a drop, too much for the average person. The Sergeant Major had a friend from long ago to whom we were introduced, and we were shown into their quite luxurious flat where we were treated like royalty, with a home-cooked meal and for me the pièce de résistance, a hot shower – HEAVEN! After a good

215

sleep, we decided the next day that a trip should be paid to the market to pick up some good bargains such as a fake Rolex and other goodies, and finishing up in the British Club where we all, with the exception of the driver, indulged in more than our fair share of alcohol, and Bud even more than me. It was on the return journey with Bud sleeping in the back of the Land Rover that I heard sounds that resembled the waste disposal unit in St Omer Barracks' Tower Block, from earlier on in my career. I realised Bud was throwing up in his sleeping bag. Of course, this could be considered a good laugh but there is always the possibility of a drunk choking on his own vomit and I kept trying to rouse Bud from his drunken stupor but he was having none of it. He was as pissed as a newt and who could blame him? Like the rest of us he had been through one hell of a three months and was only letting off steam, but there was no doubt about it, the Officer Commanding would not see it that way; so if the SSM and I could get him into the barracks undetected it would save all of us from a great deal of heartache. This we did with the minimum of fuss.

The next day we flew out of the country and I was pleased that I had not over-indulged the previous day, especially when I saw the state that Bud was in.

The flight home was fairly straight except for the moment when one of my chefs, whilst having his luggage searched, was found to have an empty 7.62mm case at the bottom of his holdall and after all the warnings that we were given on this subject I could not believe that he had been so silly. We had been told time after time that anyone found with any contraband of this kind would be in severe trouble, or in other words deeper in the shit than he had ever been. George, the culprit, managed to talk his way out of the situation and continued on his journey. I had never been able to understand George; he only had a matter of around six months to serve and his 22 years would have been up, but instead, and don't ask me why, he had volunteered to go to war. Still, I suppose each to his own, and he got home safely the same as the rest of us.

So that was the end of an episode that I will never forget. We landed at Brize Norton airfield just as we had left it three months previously, and the roar from inside the RAF Tristar was as loud as it could have been when the rubber of the massive tyres struck the runway and the engines were forced into reverse thrust. We were home and that was all that really mattered.

As the coaches pulled out of the RAF station and into the heart of the Oxfordshire countryside, even though the night had already drawn in, one of the lads, a Scotsman with a fair accent, suddenly shouted, 'Look, coos!' Of course, after seeing nothing but sand and camels for so long, the sight of

the lush vegetation and the local variety of farm
animals had us all realising just how important were
the small things that we had all missed.

Allied air-dropped propaganda leaflet

The journey back to Colchester was a long one
and it brought back memories of when as a child I
was about to embark on my annual holidays, and a
two-hour journey seemed to take an age, even
though it was a lot quicker than that. As the coach
pulled into the gates of Gujerat another loud cheer
was released and I suddenly thought that it did not
seem as if we had been away for three months. The

coach pulled to a halt on the RSM's beloved drill square and we made our way to the NAAFI bar, where all our wives and families were waiting for us, along with the local press and television. I saw then in front of me my daughter and wife running toward me and there is no doubt that that is a sight that three months before I had not been sure if I would ever see again. I could not even manage to throw a beer down my neck; all I wanted was to collect my kit and get home. This was not possible, because it was on a rather slow four-tonne truck that was at this moment trudging its way up the A12 towards Colchester, and until it arrived there was no chance of me going anywhere.

It finally arrived and I threw my kit into the back of my car, and I and my family drove through the gates ready to start a well-earned three weeks leave. I must admit that at this time I had expected to be kept hanging around for hours, but I realised that all the necessary admin had been done before we left Saudi, so here I was on the road to freedom, or as near as I could get to it anyway.

It took a hell of a long time to adjust to being able to use such luxuries as we had been used to before we left, but the worst thing for me was the way I had changed in my mental state. I knew that it would not be easy, but I had not realised just how much I would have been affected by the war itself, and I ended up seeing a psychiatrist, which apparently a lot of people in the same boat as myself also did. I still have bouts of depression but it is easing. There is no way to explain exactly how I feel during these times, but it is not what I used to be like before the Gulf conflict.

During the three weeks leave I made a visit to my parents' home, and across the driveway was an enormous board with the usual 'Welcome Home' message emblazoning the front of it. I had not until then even considered the fact that my family regarded me as the hero coming home, but here I was getting a hero's welcome, and maybe I should not have let my thoughts be swayed this way, but I really enjoyed it.

On return to work after the holiday I had to learn once again to be in control of what was for me a de luxe kitchen after the four petrol burners I had had to endure for the previous three months.

I found it increasingly hard to settle down, and when the first phase of the defence cuts were announced I applied for early redundancy. Some four months later I was called into the Officer Commanding's Office and told that I had definitely been accepted for early release, and from then on I never looked back.

While I miss some aspects of Army life, there is no way in the world after the stresses and strains of the Gulf War that I would ever consider rejoining, although in some ways I would love to relive the whole lot from the beginning.

ACC
1941 — 1991

This Certificate is Presented to

S/sgt J Rowcliffe

in recognition of valued service

with the

Army Catering Corps

and to mark the occasion of our

50th Anniversary

22nd March 1991

J. B. Bloxham, Brigadier
Director ACC

A. Collins

Lightning Source UK Ltd.
Milton Keynes UK
UKHW022255141220
375052UK00009B/840